From the Cave
to the Throne

Principles of Davidic Leadership

From the Cave to the Throne

Principles of Davidic Leadership

Jeffrey Reed

Treasure House

An Imprint of
Destiny Image® Publishers, Inc.
P.O. Box 310
Shippensburg, PA 17257-0310

"For where your treasure is,
there will your heart be also." Matthew 6:21

ISBN 1-56043-739-1

For Worldwide Distribution
Printed in the U.S.A.

This book and all other Destiny Image, Revival Press,
and Treasure House books are available
at Christian bookstores and distributors worldwide.

For a U.S. bookstore nearest you, call **1-800-722-6774**.
For more information on foreign distributors,
call **717-532-3040**.
Or reach us on the Internet: **http://www.reapernet.com**

Dedication

TO the most wonderful woman in the world, my precious wife, Tina, for her unceasing love and commitment to me, our girls, and the Kingdom of God.

TO my four daughters, Stephanie, Kendra, Tamara, and Christa.

TO my church family and staff at Power House of Deliverance Ministries, who have faithfully loved and supported me over the years.

TO my father and mother, Leroy and Romalee Reed.

TO all the men and women who have looked to me as a father/mentor; because of you, this book has come to fruition.

TO my Lord and Savior, Jesus Christ, who has made all things possible for me.

Contents

Preface

God has a place for you. He has saved you and He has given you gifts, a calling, and a purpose.

But maybe the way seems blocked right now, and you can't seem to grasp God's purpose for your life and put it into practice. Maybe you are in distress, or discontented, or in debt. If so, God has a place for you—a place of refuge, a place of training, a place of preparation, to get you ready to do the work He has for you. Let's call this place *Adullam*.

David was being pursued by Saul, who wanted to kill him. After escaping a place called Gath,

> *David therefore departed thence, and escaped to the cave Adullam: and when his brethren and all his father's house heard it, they went down thither to him. And every one that was in distress, and every one that was in debt, and every one that was discontented, gathered themselves unto him; and he became a captain over them: and there were with him about four hundred men* (1 Samuel 22:1-2).

The cave of Adullam was a place to which David ran in a time of trouble. Not only did David run there, but the Bible says other men and women knew that David was there, and they ran to the cave of Adullam also, to be with David and to make him their leader.

David had been anointed at an early age to be king of all Israel. But David didn't instantly become a great leader. You don't lie down a blunder and wake up a wonder. When God puts an anointing on your life, it will take *time* for that anointing to develop, and it will take *time* for you as a person to catch up with your anointing. Maybe David could have successfully accepted the kingship when he was anointed, but God waited until David was 30 years old. There were things in David's life that needed to be worked out, things that needed to be worked up, and things that needed to be worked in. God allowed time for David to become ready.

When David ran to Adullam, not only his brethren and his father's house went down to him, but so did everyone who was in distress, everyone who was in debt, and everyone who was discontented. We have the same kind of people in the Church today. If you are not distressed, you are in debt. If you are not in debt, you are discontented. Maybe you are all three.

Those four hundred men who were in distress, or discontented, or in debt, ran to David. With his skill as a leader, David trained them to be versatile warriors. When David was through with them, they were able to throw rocks with their right hand as well as with their left and accurately hit a target.

Adullam was a type of Calvary. We were in spiritual debt when we ran to Calvary. We were dissatisfied and discontented with life. We were rejected and insignificant and unimportant.

But God picked us up and made something out of us. When we walked away from Calvary, we were somebody.

David sent those four hundred men out against nations. They fought thousands of foot soldiers—trained, skilled men of war—and killed and destroyed them. In addition, the same four hundred men who had gone out would return. That seems irrational and unreal, like a fairy tale. How could four hundred men go out against thousands of soldiers and come back shouting, "We got the victory! We got the spoil!" without one of the four hundred being killed, while they themselves killed thousands? How did that happen? David had poured himself into them, and it all started in the cave of Adullam. That's where David began to build their character, to show them their worth, to show them who they were, and to show them their purpose. By tapping into their hidden potential, their hidden possibilities, David made these men and women begin to feel good about themselves. David taught them something: You don't have to be dissatisfied with life. You don't have to be under the burden and the stress of death. You don't have to be in debt.

Then those men went out and destroyed other nations, took wealth from sinners, and paid off their own debts. But it all began with their experience in the cave of Adullam. David, as their leader, encouraged them and built them up, letting them know that they were worth something.

We ourselves are in a war. We are in a spiritual war. The Bible says we are not ignorant concerning the devices of the devil (see 2 Cor. 2:11). Scripture tells us to put on the whole armor of God so that we will be able to stand against the wiles of the devil (see Eph. 6).

I want you to know that you are worth something. I want to build your self-esteem. I want to tap into your hidden potential, those secret possibilities that you don't even know are there, and trigger your gifts to make them surface and come to life. Then you will find yourself functioning and flourishing in your ministry, in the hope of your calling, as never before. You will find yourself being motivated and you will find yourself being stirred. Like David and the four hundred, you will find yourself achieving what God has called you to do, and you will find yourself falling in love with your Master over and over again every day.

Chapter 1

One Body

If we hope to see change in the Church and in the world, we have to have *unity*. We have to accept responsibility for one another. Not only does the pastor have to accept responsibility for his congregation, but the people have to accept responsibility for their pastor. When we accept responsibility for one another, and are part of one another, we will have an awesome power to change ourselves and to change the Church.

Where does the power come from?

A while ago I was cutting some wood at my house with an electric saw. I had used it all day, but suddenly, when I went to cut another piece of wood, I pushed the button and nothing happened. When a saw doesn't come on, the first thing you do is check and see if it is plugged in. I went to the wall socket and, sure enough, the plug was hanging out. It wasn't connected all the way. So I pushed it in and went back to the saw, and when I pushed the button the saw came on. Unless it was connected to its source of power, it couldn't do its job. As long as we are connected to the source, we can run and function in the hope of our calling. That saw was created to cut wood. That's all it was created to do. It must be connected in order to function.

Every one of us was created for a purpose. Nobody just exists; nobody is just here; nobody is just hanging out. We each have our own personality, our own individuality, our own identity. We have an objective in sight. We have a destiny to walk into. We have a calling to fulfill. Once we understand that and grasp that in our hearts and in our minds, we are going to be an awesome people on the face of the earth.

But to be an awesome people, we have to know who we are, not just as individuals, but as a people.

Bones and Flesh

After the Philistines killed Saul and his sons, and the Lord turned the kingdom of Israel over to David, "All Israel gathered themselves to David unto Hebron, saying, Behold, we are thy bone and thy flesh" (1 Chron. 11:1). That sounds like a marriage covenant, doesn't it?

From the beginning, God has always used men. Sometimes we have a problem with that, because we honor the ones who are over us, and there's a danger that we might try to make a god out of a man. Or, just as likely, we find out that the people over us are not enough like God. But the fact remains that God chooses to use men, and He chose to use David.

The word *Israel* means one that rules as God. Israel was going to be the example, the model, the ideal. Of all the nations, God spoke to Israel. "I didn't choose you because you were many," He told them. "I chose you because you were few. But I'm going to raise you up and you are going to be the ideal of all the nations. I'm going to set you on a pedestal. I'm going to glorify you. I'm going to turn the light of Heaven on you. I'm going to make you the head and not the tail. I'm going to place you above and not beneath. I'm going to make you to lend and not to borrow. I'm going to use you as a pattern, as a role model, as an ideal."

Israel was chosen, but Israel was in trouble. They were at war with the Philistines—and they were losing. The king of Israel, along with his sons, had just been killed. Israel needed to hang together at this time; Israel needed somebody to gather around. They gathered around David. There is something significant in the word *gathered*. Notice that David didn't call a board meeting. He didn't call a summit. Israel voluntarily gathered around David.

After David killed Goliath, the Israelites slaughtered the Philistines, but David received credit for the victory because he had killed the first and biggest. When David and Saul were returning from this battle, "the women came out of all cities of Israel, singing and dancing...and said, Saul hath slain his thousands, and David his ten thousands" (1 Sam. 18:6b-7). The people loved David.

Because David behaved himself wisely, all Israel went to David when he arrived in Hebron. Hebron means "communion." It means "fellowship." All Israel came to a place of fellowship and communion with God, with each other, and with David. This was years after the four hundred men had gathered with him in the cave of Adullam. In his down times, only a few had gathered with him.

In an hour of victory, it is easy for a leader to find people to gather around him. But it doesn't matter whether our leaders are having times of victory or times of defeat. We as a people, in our local assemblies, need to gather around our local pastors and let them know we are with them. We are all part of one body, and we need to tell them what the Israelites told David: "We are thy bone and thy flesh."

I want to encourage pastors and leaders. People are going to gather around you as never before, because we are coming into the last move of God. God is raising up people who are yearning and looking for something, looking to belong, and they are going to gather around their Davids. All you have to do is just get to Hebron. God will send them to Hebron, to where you are. We just need to get into fellowship and communion.

We need to get into Hebron not only for one year, or two or three years; we need to get into Hebron and know that we are going to stay there. We need to get into Hebron and know that God is there with us. We need to get into Hebron and develop a relationship, an intimacy with God, and God will cause the people to gather.

The Spirit of David

David was the only man to whom God said, "I'm going to establish your throne forever." He said, "Israel, you have been lacking; you have been tossed; you have been beaten; you have been rejected; you have been from nation to nation. But I'm going to raise up My servant David and he is going to shepherd you." David's throne is eternal. Jesus inherited it, and even down to this generation, God is still raising up heirs to the throne and putting the spirit of David upon leaders.

People will gather to leaders who have David's spirit. There was something about David's character that attracted people. The very Hebrew word for "gather" means not to call people together, but for people to be attracted to someone. We are gathering to leaders with David's spirit because we are attracted to them. We see something in them; we want to be like them.

God has promised to provide His people with David's spirit of leadership.

> *And I will set up one shepherd over them, and he shall feed them, even My servant David; he shall feed them, and he shall be their shepherd. And I the Lord will be their God, and My servant David a prince among them...I will raise up for them a plant of renown* (Ezekiel 34:23-24a,29a).

"A plant of renown" means somebody who has a great reputation. David was loved by Israel, and he was loved by God. "I love David because of his praise. I rejoice in his worship. I love him because of the way he walks. He has a heart that pursues Me." It is time that we gathered around our Davids. It is time that we told our local assemblies and local pastors, "We are thy bone and thy flesh." It is time for pastors to demonstrate that they have inherited the spirit of David, that they have a heart after God.

Genesis 49:10 talks about a gathering of the people at Shiloh, which means "a place of rest." This was a place of rest for the Israelites, and a shadow of the rest to come. David was also a shadow of the Shiloh to come—Jesus being the actual substance. When the people gathered around David, he was only a reflection of the Lord Jesus Christ. He was a shadow of the real thing to come.

We know that God is still raising up Davids in our midst, and that the spirit of David still rests upon pastors, because St. James, in a meeting of the apostles in Jerusalem, said, "As it is written, After this I will return, and will build again the tabernacle of David" (Acts 15:15b-16a).

So when we tell our pastors, "we are thy bone and thy flesh," what are we saying? Bones give the body structure—they are the skeleton. One function of the bones is that they provide structural support for the mechanical action of tissue, such as contraction of muscles and expansion of the lungs. When Israel said to David, "we are thy bone," they were actually saying, "David, we are going to support your action and your cause."

Do you feel that way about your local church and your local pastor? Are you plugged in, or are you *almost* plugged in? Are you connected? Are you there saying, "Pastor, we are going to support your action and we are going to support your cause"? I tell my congregation all the time that God gives the vision to the pastor. "Let God give me the vision," I tell them. "You help me bring the vision to pass."

We as a people have to be so connected with the pastor, or the one who is head over us, that we say, "We are going to support your cause and we are going to support your actions." Don't question his actions. Don't play down his actions. Say, "Whatever he does, we're going to support that."

Another function of the bone is to protect soft parts. God created your brain and He put it inside a protective case. God created a heart and He put it behind protective bones. The bone structure around these soft tissues guards them from harm. In following our leaders, we should say, "We are going to protect you until the end." The Israelites' attitudes were "If David falls, if David dies, what is the use of going on?"

Second Samuel 21:15 describes one battle against the Philistines that David fought until he was exhausted. One of Goliath's sons, Ishbibenob, came after David with a spear and a sword to kill him. Abishai saw this and came to David's aid, and killed Ishbibenob. Abishai stood in the gap. When he saw David about to be slain, Abishai forgot about his own family. He forgot about his living. He forgot about his children at home. He forgot about the clothes he was wearing. He forgot about everything he had, and he put his life on the line to stand in the gap and protect his leader.

That is what it means to be bone and flesh of someone you love. You forget about everything else. When I say, "I'm your bone," I'm willing to put my life on the line for yours. This is what Jesus did for us. What manner of love is this that a man lay down his life for his friend? That is what Abishai did. He put his life on the line for his friend. His actions said, "Whether I live or die, I just want to let you know I'm putting my life on the line for you. Whether I get the victory or whether I go down, I just want you to know that I hung in there with you until the end."

Let me say this to leaders and pastors: God in this hour is going to give us some men and women who are committed to our cause, who are going to support our actions. They are going to put their lives on the line.

Somebody will say, "We should do this."

These people say, "No, what did the pastor say?"

"Should we go here?"

"No. What did the pastor say?"

I hear this in my church, and it's not that I'm taking away their individuality or their identity, it is just that they recognize that God has set up a man in their midst, a man who is connected with God, a man to whom God has given a vision, to lead them.

"We don't want to move away from David," the Israelites would say. "David has the vision. He knows our destiny. He knows where God is leading us. We don't want to step out of rank."

"We want to stand in there," people should say today, "and whatever the pastor says, that's what we are going to do. Wherever the pastor says to go, that's where we are going. Whatever the pastor says, we will promise to do."

Another thing bones do is to provide a protected place for specialized tissue such as the bone marrow, which forms the blood. David was like the bone marrow of Israel, forming the lifeblood of Israel. After Abishai killed Goliath's son, he said to David, "You're not going into battle with us any more. You almost put out the light of Israel." Isn't that an awesome statement to make to your leader? "You are going to stay in Jerusalem, because you almost put out the lifeline, the light of Israel. If the light goes out, we're going to walk in darkness. If the light goes out, what is the use of living? If the light goes out, what is the use of fighting any longer? You are the one through whom God channels His anointing and His blessing."

I want you to be connected more in your local assembly. I want you to be more supportive. I want you to do more. The man of God in your midst holds the Word, basically eternal life. When someone is anointed by God, his word has authority.

God's Word to Leaders

Elijah had God's word in him. Elijah went and stood before Ahab, the king, and told him, "It's not going to rain until I say so." It's mind-boggling that a man could stop the heavens from producing water. But God has to give the man the word. You don't make a god out of the man. You just honor the man and stay with the one whom God has set up over you.

There is a lesson here for leaders. After Elijah said it wasn't going to rain, God told him to hide himself. "Go hide yourself by the brook" (see 1 Kings 17:1-3). Many times, spiritual famine is going to come into our lives. We are going to have dry times in leadership. We're going to have valley experiences. But not all dry times and down times are bad times.

As a fisherman, there were times when I had a great harvest of fish. But I also had to take the nets out of the water, bring the nets to the shore, and mend the holes in the nets. It seemed like a dry time, because I wasn't catching anything, but it was a time of mending, a time of building again, a time of re-energizing.

Ask a farmer. There are times in the farmer's life when he is out plowing and planting, out reaping and sowing, but there comes a time when he parks his machinery in the barn, changes the oil, fills it up with gas, puts new filters in it, puts air in the tires, and patches holes. It may seem like a down time, but it is not a bad time; it is a necessary time.

Sometimes God takes us in, calls us aside, and says, "Hide thyself that I might work on you." Sometimes leaders have to give God time aside for Him to work on us.

Later, God spoke to Elijah and said, "Show thyself." This was a time of restoration. He gained great victory. He gained a great triumph in the anointing of God. God restored Israel to Himself. After we hide ourselves, we have to show ourselves.

We also have to behave ourselves. Israel loved David so much because David behaved himself wisely. After David killed Goliath, he could have been filled with pride. He could have said, "I'm the leader now because I am anointed." But David went back and served under Saul as Saul's armorbearer.

Just because you kill a Goliath, don't think you are going to walk in victory and triumph and just kill every giant that comes your way. Stay humble. There will be times when you are going to grow faint. Then you will need an Abishai to rescue you.

Abishai said to David, "You almost put out the light of Israel." Later, when Absalom took the throne and David was getting ready to recapture the throne, David spoke to his men and said, "Joab, I want you to go this way. Abishai, you go this way. I'll go this way." And all the men got together and said, "David, you're not going out. You are worth ten thousand of us." David's men were connected to him. They said, "If they kill us out there, we will just be dead. But if they kill you out there, where will the kingdom go?"

That kind of attitude puts a big responsibility on leaders. When people begin to realize their function under leadership, and leaders begin to realize their function in the people of God, we're going to accomplish some things.

What People Need

People today are looking for effective leadership—somebody who produces results, somebody who can get the job done. This is why God said, "I will raise up for them a plant of renown." He is going to raise up leaders with great character and great reputations, who are able to get the job done.

As leaders, we have a responsibility to perfect the saints of God. We have to take the nobodies, the rejects, the disorderly, people with low self-esteem, people who don't care about life, people who just let life pass by. We have to take those people and perfect them. Not only do we have to perfect the saints, but we have to edify the Body of Christ.

One meaning of edify is to "polish and bring to an elegant finish." When I was in New Orleans, I sat down on a shoeshine stool. My shoes had a little dirt on them. The shine had grown dull. But the man pulled out his shoeshine things and he began to put on polish and water, and he took the brush and rubbed them, and took the rag and wiped them. When I looked down at my shoes, they were different. He had taken something that had gotten dull and brought it to an elegant finish. He had polished it. And this is what we have to do in the lives of our people. We are to take those lives that are torn, take those lives that are dirty, and polish them until they come to an elegant finish. God can hold them up and say, "This is mine."

When we're trying to bring people to an elegant finish, we have to be careful about our own finish. As leaders, we become people's ideal. We become people's example. So we have to give attention to ourselves. Now, a lot of people talk about our need as Christians to get rid of self. Put self under your feet. But there are a lot of good things about self. I love myself. You might think that is vain. But I can't love you unless I love myself. The Bible says, "Love your neighbor as yourself." So you need to be in love with yourself in order to give love to someone else. In this hour, we need to have some self-worth. We need to know that we are worth something.

Another thing we need to have is self-confidence. Scripture tells us to be "confident of this very thing, that He which hath begun a good work in you will perform it until the day of Jesus Christ" (Phil. 1:6). He will complete it. If He started on me, He's not going to leave me unfinished. He's going to complete me and perfect me and bring me to an elegant finish.

We also should build into our character the trait of being a self-starter. Get some initiative. Be a hustler. Be a worker. Daniel said that "people that do know their God shall be strong, and do exploits" (Dan. 11:32b). We do know our God, and we're not just standing on the sidelines waiting to get into the midst of the battle; we're already on the field performing and functioning in the hope of our calling. We know what we are called to do. We're not just waiting for our part in the battle, although we may be waiting for a special anointing to come into bloom. Yet, while we're in the battle we are still working on ourselves, developing ourselves. We have things we have to work on.

Leaders need to practice self-sacrifice, denying ourselves for others. We need that in our character.

We as a people need self-esteem. Scripture says, "I am fearfully and wonderfully made..." (Ps. 139:14). Have you ever stopped at that verse and seen what God is saying about you? You are tremendous. You are terrific. It doesn't matter what others think about you. God said you're tremendous. God said you're a terrific individual. People will look down their nose at you. They will pass you over and count you as insignificant and say that you are unimportant, but God says you are tremendous and terrific.

We need self-control. We need to have a balance, maintain our dignity, hold onto our integrity. Scripture says the devil came to Job and wanted to steal his integrity. God told the devil, "Look, after all you've done to Job, he still maintains his integrity." In the midst of trials, in the midst of storms, in the midst of valleys, no matter what I may go through, I'm going to hold onto my integrity. I'm going to stay steadfast. I'm going to remain immovable.

We need to build self-respect into our characters. There is nothing wrong with being a David. When Samuel came to Bethlehem, David wasn't invited to the feast, as all his brothers were. They thought he was unimportant, and they sent him to the fields. Have you ever had people pass you by, overlook your anointing, overlook who you are, look down their nose at you, and just send you away rejected?

When Samuel saw Eliab, he said, "Certainly the anointed of God stands before me."

But God said, "No. You are looking through the eyes of man." So Samuel went through the seven sons of Jesse, and God said, "None of these is him."

Samuel turned to Jesse and asked him, "Do you have another son?"

"Yes, he is in the field. He smells like the sheep. He's out there playing his harp."

Samuel said, "Send for him." When David walked into the room, smelling like sheep, God said, "That's the one."

David was the eighth son of Jesse. The number eight means a new beginning. It signifies the dawning of a new day. When God brought David in, it signified that God wanted to bring about a new day in Israel.

People may look at you and see a shepherd boy. God sees a king. It doesn't matter how people see us. It matters how God sees us. People may say you think of yourself too highly. If I am thinking of myself too highly, forgive me, but I am still somebody. There was a time in my life when I was a nobody. I was not a child of God. I was not born again. I was a heathen. I was alienated from the covenants of Israel. But now, I am in a covenant relationship. I am somebody.

It is right to know that we are somebody, but sometimes we get it into our minds that our pastor is no better than we are. "He puts on his pants the same way I put on my pants," you might think. "He sits at the table and eats just as I eat." Some of you treat your pastor like a can of Coke. You go to the machine, put money in there, get the Coke, pop the lid off, drink the soda, and throw the can away. But somebody may come by and see worth in the very thing you threw away, and bring the can down to the recycling place, because it is worth something. Stop draining the substance and throwing away the vessel. Treasure them both, the substance and the vessel.

That is what David wanted to do with the covenant. Uzzah touched the ark of the covenant and God killed him for it, so David was afraid to bring the ark to Jerusalem. He just wanted to set it aside. Obed-edom stood up and said, "If you don't want it, give it to me. I'll take it. Bring it into my house. I don't care if it kills somebody." The same thing that kills has the ability to bring life, and the ability to bless. Obed-edom was blessed the whole time the ark was in his house. Don't just use your pastor, in whom the Word of God has been planted. If you don't want the can, give it to me.

We have to esteem our brothers and sisters in the church, too. God has placed His Spirit in them, so don't treat them like soda cans and throw them away. Esteem them, even if they're in bad condition.

Job had boils, lost his children, lost all his possessions, and then his friends came by to comfort him and said, "You are worthless." Job said, "I'm not inferior to you. I might be in bad condition, and I might not look good, and I might be going through my winter season. But I'm not inferior to you. See, after a while this is going to pass."

Whatever situation you are in, it is going to pass after a while. While you are in the midst of it, don't look down on yourself and feel inferior to anybody. In turn, don't look down on those who are in a bad condition.

One of the best definitions of success is "doing the very best at what you are called to do." If you do the very best at what you are called to do, you don't have to feel inferior to anybody. Just know that you are doing your best. Don't stop at good. Do people ever do something for you and say, "This is good enough"? Don't stop at good. Let your good become better. Let your better become best. And then function on that plane and do your very best for God.

I am an engineer by trade, and in the midst of working as an engineer, I learned to lay bricks. One day God gave me this parable of a bricklayer:

A bricklayer received a contract for a project. Before he went out to the job site to set up everything, the bricklayer called all his tools together and said, "Do you know your function?"

The mortar mixer jumped up and said, "Yes, my job is to mix mortar."

The wheelbarrow stood up and said, "My job is to carry bricks and mortar to the wall."

The ruler said, "My job is to measure out the wall."

The line stood up and said, "My job is to keep the wall straight horizontally."

The level said, "My job is to make sure the wall is straight."

The saw stood up and said, "Yes, sir, Mister Bricklayer. My job is to cut the bricks into shape."

The trowel stood up and said, "My job is to spread mortar."

And the bricklayer said, "Since all of you know your job, we are going to load up and go down to the job site." Down at the job site, the bricklayer stepped out of his truck and said, "All right, mortar mixer, I want you to mix some mortar. And, wheelbarrow, carry some bricks to the wall. And, ruler, I want you to measure out the wall."

Before the bricklayer could say anything else, the mortar mixer stopped him and said, "Listen, I can't mix any mortar until you fill me."

And the wheelbarrow said, "I can't carry any bricks to the wall unless you push me."

The line said, "I can't keep the wall straight unless you connect me."

The ruler said, "I can't measure out the wall unless you unfold me."

The level said, "I can't keep the wall straight unless you hold me."

And the saw said, "I can't cut the bricks unless you turn me on."

The trowel said, "I can't spread your mortar unless you put your hand on me."

After all the tools had made their complaint, the bricklayer looked at them with a smile on his face and said, "Although each one of you was designed and created for a purpose, you can't perform unless you are in my hands and I use you."

Statement of truth: It's only His touch that causes me to perform in the purposes I was created for.

People are looking for leaders who show that God is with them. But have you ever thought about what leaders look for in you?

What Leaders Need

After Moses died, God raised up Joshua to be the leader. The people said to Joshua, "We are going to do what you say as long as God is with you. Whatever you say, we will do. Where you send us, we will go. As we hearkened unto Moses, so will we hearken unto you" (see Josh. 1:16-17). They totally submitted to Joshua.

When you become bone of your pastor's bone and flesh of your pastor's flesh, victory is promoted in the local assembly. The Israelites knew that. Exodus 17:8 records an Amalekite attack. In the next verse we read, "Moses said...." Then "Joshua did...." Moses responded to the crisis, and Joshua did exactly as Moses decided.

As long as Moses held his hands up, the Israelites were winning the battle (see Ex. 17:11). Can't you hear him saying, "I have my hands up, and then I put them down because I am exhausted. I have them up again, and then I put them down again. As long as I keep them up we win. I drop them and we lose." People came to the aid of their pastor. They brought a rock and sat him down on it. One got under one arm and one got under the other, and they held up the hands of their leader. They were connected with leadership. They realized that as long as the leader's hands were up, they were going to win. "Let's connect ourselves," they said.

"Let's become one. Let's become bone. Let's become flesh." God saw. He promised that He Himself would fight against the Amalekites until they were wiped out. Praise broke out in the camp because of the victory that God had just given them.

When leaders and people function together, it promotes victory. We've been divided too long. We've been separated too long. We've been at one another's throats too long. It is time to gather ourselves together under the spirit of David so that victory might be promoted.

A Gathering to Modern Davids

There was a group of people who came and said to David, "We are your helpers in warfare. We are with you because God has anointed you" (see 1 Chron. 12:18). In the Body of Christ, in the local assembly, we need some people to be helpers.

The men who joined David included men who were mighty in warfare (see 1 Chron. 11:10). Others joined because they knew what Israel ought to do. They *knew*. They weren't guessing, they weren't speculating, but they knew the direction Israel should go in. Some joined who were skillful in warfare (see 1 Chron. 12:1). Some could keep rank (see 1 Chron. 12:38).

In this hour, God is sending us some people who are going to be helpers in warfare. God is sending us some people who are going to be mighty in warfare. God is sending us some people who are going to be skillful in warfare. God is sending us men and women who will keep rank.

There was a master builder who wanted to build a pulpit. He was getting his tools together when he heard a commotion in his tool box. He looked in and said, "That sounds just like things in the church."

He heard the plane tell the hammer, "We have to get rid of you. You make too much noise."

Then the hammer spoke back and said, "If you get rid of me you are going to have to get rid of the sandpaper, because it is always rubbing people the wrong way."

And the sandpaper said, "If you get rid of me, you are going to have to get rid of the plane, because it just works on the surface. It doesn't have any depth to it."

The plane said, "Well, if you get rid of me, you are going to have to get rid of the screwdriver, because it has to turn round and round before it gets anything accomplished."

The screwdriver said, "If you get rid of me, you're going to have to get rid of the saw, because it is always cutting people off."

The master builder was watching and listening to all their complaining, bickering, and fussing.

Then the saw said, "If you get rid of me, you're going to have to get rid of the master builder, because he is the only one who can gather all of us together and build the pulpit."

The master builder completed the pulpit with all of those bickering tools, with all those tools that couldn't get along. He brought them together.

Then he stepped into the pulpit and spoke these words: "The Spirit of the Lord God is upon me. He has anointed me to preach the Gospel unto the poor. It was the Spirit of God that brought us together. It is the Spirit of God that makes us work beside one another. It is the Spirit of God that gets rid of all our complaints. It is the Spirit of God that makes us one. It is the Spirit of God that makes us bone of each other's bone. It is the Spirit of God that makes us flesh of one another's flesh. It is the Spirit of God that bonds us together. It is the glue that holds us together. We have a job to do. We have something to build. We have a kingdom to display. We have an anointing to show. But it's got to be by the Spirit of God."

Did you not know it is the Spirit of God that takes those dry bones and asks the preacher, "Can these bones live?" It is the Spirit of God that speaks to the preacher and says, "Speak to Me. I'll take the separated ones. I'll take the rejected ones. I'll take the low-down ones. I'll take the no-good ones. I'll take the nobodies. I'll resurrect them and give them life, and join them together and make them stand up." It is the Spirit of God that brings all the people together to accomplish His purpose.

It is the Spirit of God that brings all of our different personalities together and molds us into a body and says, "I'm going to get glory from that." It was the Spirit of God that filled the Church on the day of Pentecost and made them one. It is the Spirit of God that welds us together. It doesn't matter what denomination we belong to. It doesn't matter how tall, how short, how wide, or how thin we are. God is able to bring us together, weld us together, and give us a job to do.

Chapter 2

Taking Heed to Ourselves

There was a young boy who built a toy boat. After finishing his boat, he added a sail and attached a piece of string to it. He took it down to the water and the wind began to push the boat gently through the water. After a while, a strong gust arose and pushed the boat until the string broke. The boy ran along the bank, hoping the wind would push the boat ashore, but it only pushed it further away. Finally it was out of sight.

Weeks later, as the young boy was walking around downtown, he looked into a store window and saw his boat with a price tag on it. He rushed home and emptied his piggy bank until he had enough to buy the boat. After purchasing it, he walked out of the store and said to the boat, "You are twice mine. You were mine when I made you, and you are mine because I bought you."

Even as the boat was twice the boy's, so we believers are twice God's. Man was made as the crown of God's creation.

Because He created us in His image and made us in His likeness, we are His. But sin separated us from God.

Yet God showed His love toward us in that while we were yet sinners, Christ died for us, so that all things might pass away and so that all things might become new (see 2 Cor. 5:17). Therefore I am not my own; I have been purchased with the blood of Jesus (see 1 Cor. 6:19-20). My body is the temple of the Holy Ghost. We are His because He made us, and we are His because He purchased us. The most important thing we have to realize is to whom we belong. Knowing *whose* we are is just as important as knowing *who* we are.

Many Scriptures tell us to take heed to ourselves. We find one example in First Timothy 4:16. "Take heed unto thyself, and unto the doctrine...." When the Bible says, "Take heed unto thyself," it usually means "Be careful about this" or "Pay attention" or "Watch yourself on this." We must be careful to know whose we are. There are only two spirits we can belong to in this world. We belong either to the Spirit of God or to the spirit of the devil.

When you were growing up, did you ever get lost? Did you ever get separated from the other kids and ask yourself, "Where am I? How do I find my way home?" It's very unsettling not to know the way home. We want to have a place to go back to. We need a place where we belong. When you were out playing with the other kids, and it started to get dark, and everybody started heading home to dinner, wasn't it good to know that you had a home to go to also? You had parents you belonged with.

We want to know that we have a home, that we belong somewhere. As adults, we recognize the reality of death more, and realize that our home in this world is only temporary. Also, the more we mature in the Lord, the more we hunger and thirst for His holiness, the less we feel at home in this world. We want to know that there's another home to go back to, and we want to be sure we know the way home.

We see many people out there who don't even know who they are, who don't know they have a purpose, who don't know the Lord. They don't have any confidence that there is an eternal home waiting for them, or if they do have confidence, it is misplaced.

But we as believers not only know who we are, we know whose we are. Many people say, "I'm a child of God like you." But we did not come into being as sons and daughters of Almighty God. We were purchased and adopted. We know that if we have the Spirit of Christ in us, we are His; because we are His, He takes care of us throughout life. He gives us purpose. He feeds us and clothes us. His home is ours. We will sit with Him at His table. He will do the best for us and give us the best. The only thing that stops us and hinders us from getting the best is ourselves.

We Can Be Who We Want to Be

You can be just about anything you want to be. You can accomplish just about anything you want to accomplish. God has put something inside you that makes you able to accomplish anything you want to do. God established laws here on earth, such as the law of gravity. But God put something inside us that enables us to defy the law of gravity. God has given us a creative mind, so that if we want to do it, we can.

Flip Wilson played a character on television who always said, "The devil made me do it." It was funny because the character was just making an excuse. But people try to use that for a real excuse. Don't you know that nobody can *make* you do anything? They can't. People can suggest things. The power of suggestion has a great influence. Sometimes even in the Church you find people who try to control you, who try to manipulate you. But the people who get manipulated and the people who get controlled are the people who don't know who they are and the people who don't know whose they are.

Get Into Win-Win Situations

When we really know who we are, we will listen to people's opinions, but we will recognize that their opinions are just opinions. We won't be manipulated. We won't be controlled by somebody who is in a stronger position. We are already in touch with God through His Word and His Holy Spirit, so we have standards by which to judge opinions.

The Bible asks, "Can two walk together, except they be agreed?" (Amos 3:3). Before agreeing with people, we can look to see whether their opinion is in agreement with the Word of the Lord. If we don't know what is in the Word of God, we can be manipulated by somebody whose opinion sounds good. But not every opinion that sounds good is right.

Now, not every difference of opinion can be clearly settled by looking at the Word of God. There are some differing opinions that are not good or bad, they are just different. If you say something and the deacon does not agree with you, then the deacon should be man enough to say, "No, I don't agree with you." Saying that he doesn't agree with you doesn't mean he will try to manipulate you to agree with him. You can agree to disagree agreeably. You both win.

But if you and the deacon don't agree, and he gives in and says, "Well, maybe it will work; maybe it is right," but inside he doesn't feel peace about it, then he shouldn't go along, because the Bible says, "Let the peace of God rule in your hearts" (Col. 3:15a). Then you win, but he loses.

At other times, because you know the personality or motivation of a brother or sister, you might lose just so that brother or sister can win.

Then there are lose-lose situations. You say, "I'm going to have my way no matter what." Unfortunately, you will find this in a lot of marriages. Both husband and wife are stubborn. Both insist that their way is the only way to get something done and are unwilling to compromise. They are also unwilling to consider the value of the other's opinion. So nothing gets done. Both lose.

The Bible says, "Let this mind be in you, which was also in Christ Jesus" (Phil. 2:5). A brother and a sister might have good ideas—excellent ideas. But we can't do both of their ideas. So what happens if they both yield their ideas to the mind of Christ, which is on a higher level? Both of them win. If they both care more about the mind of Christ than about their own ideas, then both will be happy with the result, whatever it is.

If we would do this more, we would find better marriages. We would find more people who are stable, who don't feel pressured to yield their will to another's opinion, and who aren't threatened by yielding their will to someone who has a better idea. Suppose a wife wants to watch a movie. The husband says, "No, I don't feel like watching a movie. Maybe we ought to go to a game."

"All right." But she really doesn't feel like going to a game and her husband doesn't really feel like watching a movie.

If they look beyond their own desires they can meet on another level. They can look for a way to please both. "Say, why don't we go for a walk on the beach?"

"O.K." They don't do what either one first wanted, because the wife would have been bored at the game, and the husband would have fallen asleep watching the movie. Both of them enjoy walking on the beach. Both of them win.

We have to learn to work this into our character—not only to be sensitive to other people, but to be sensitive and honest with ourselves. Make sure you are not just doing things to manipulate or control other people.

A Spirit of Control

Many times there is a spirit of witchcraft in churches. Now when we think of witchcraft, we think of potions and spells. But the main thing about witchcraft is *control*. That is why God said, "If you find any witches in the land, kill them." Some saints say they believe in the power of witchcraft. I don't. The Bible says, "Greater is He that is in you, than he that is in the world" (1 Jn. 4:4b). But many times, because you hear about things that happened to other people, you become fearful. No weapon formed against you shall prosper if you put God first.

The spirit of witchcraft is nothing but the spirit of Jezebel. Jezebel was a witch. She didn't use potions or voodoo. She loved to be in control. Jezebel loved to have titles. She loved to be around power.

When Ahab wanted Naboth's vineyard and couldn't get it, he laid on his bed and cried like a baby. "What's the matter, boy?" Jezebel asked.

"I wanted the vineyard of Naboth but he won't sell it because he got it from his father."

"Don't worry," she said. "Get up and eat. Don't worry about a thing." She was controlling. She had Naboth killed. Ahab was king, but she controlled him.

You can see this spirit of Jezebel getting into the Church: people trying to control each other to get their own way, or sometimes just for a feeling of security. Cliques represent a Jezebel spirit. When you see a clique, somebody is in charge. That is the spirit of witchcraft, because it is controlling. The suggestions made by the one in control, or her opinions about something, weigh heavily on the people in that clique. They might get together and talk about some other woman. Somebody in the clique who doesn't even know that woman will say things about her and begin to despise her without ever getting to know her. That is the spirit of witchcraft, because the clique is now controlling someone's thoughts about somebody else.

In the house of the Lord, we don't want our thoughts controlled by anybody except the Spirit of the Living God. "Let this mind be in you, which was also in Christ Jesus" (Phil. 2:5). When we live according to the pattern of God's Word, everything will work well in the Body of Christ.

Scripture says that God establishes offices in the Church: first apostles, then prophets, then evangelists, pastors, and teachers, "for the perfecting of the saints, for the work of ministry, for the edifying of the body of Christ: Till we all come in the unity of the faith, and of the knowledge of the Son of God, unto a perfect man, unto the measure of the stature of the fulness of Christ" (Eph. 4:11-13).

Apostles, prophets, evangelists, pastors, and teachers are there to direct us. If anybody in the Church is manipulating or controlling you and saying something other than what these leaders are saying, you need to beware of a controlling spirit. If anything goes contrary to the divine order and setup of God, it is out of God's will and we need to take heed unto ourselves. If we get outside God's order it will be our own doing. It will be because we did not have order in the Church, because we were manipulated by somebody. There is nothing wrong with listening. There is nothing wrong with taking instruction. You can take instruction and not be manipulated or controlled by somebody. You can still be under the control and direction of the Holy Spirit.

We may come under someone's control because we respect that person. But we must be sure that anyone trying to influence us is saying what the Church says. God "is no respecter of persons" (Acts 10:34b). His salvation is available to everyone, and everyone must go along with His rules.

Reach Out to All

We appreciate people. We love people. But to respect one over another is to be a respecter of persons. We need to be available to help everyone. Many of the teenage girls who show up at our church are confused and badly in need of direction. Don't look down your nose at them. If we don't catch them now, you know what's out there waiting for them. That's why it's important for some of the women, who are saintly and know how to live right, to pull these girls aside and impart some of their wisdom to them. Otherwise, they are going to be lost. They are going to make the same mistakes you made while growing up. We don't need to learn by making mistakes. We can learn from the experience of others. Take these girls aside and teach them. Pour out your heart. Be a mother figure. Be a woman of God around these girls and let them know the way to go.

The same is true with the young men coming in. If we don't throw our arms around them and love them and show them something better than what is out there, we're going to lose them.

We can't be a respecter of persons when it comes to reaching out. People come into church who do not practice proper hygiene. We don't want to be around them. We hug everybody else, but with these we just shake hands, keeping our distance, because they smell. That is not the way to do it. Take them aside and let them know. You have to do it in love. If we don't do it, then the world looks at them and laughs. The world doesn't want to be around them. The saints don't want to be around them. So they are rejected people. The Church is where they are supposed to come in and be accepted.

You'll find people who can't balance a checkbook. Teach them. You'll find people who make bad decisions and bad choices. Help them. This is all in taking heed to ourselves. There is so much work to be done in the house of the Lord, but we always put it off and wait for somebody else to do it. We've got to take heed unto ourselves.

You need to look at yourself as a copying machine. You've got to duplicate what you've learned and impart it to others. You've got to duplicate the maturity and wisdom that is in you. The anointing God has put in you, He also wants in somebody else.

Why don't we share what we have? Maybe we are ashamed of the gospel. St. Paul said, "I am not ashamed of the gospel of Christ: for it is the power of God unto salvation..." (Rom. 1:16). He was a radical person; that attitude made him go and stand before kings.

What kind of person should I be if I'm going to duplicate myself? If you ever get radical about the gospel, you'll begin to tell yourself, "I'm not ashamed. I've got to tell somebody about it. I've got to tell them in love. I've got to extend mercy. I've got to show compassion. That's the type person I've got to be." We have to become that type of person, and God will do something in us and for us. We are commissioned to go into all the world and spread the gospel.

What kind of person should I be? First Timothy 4:12 helps us answer that question. First of all, "Let no man despise thy youth." Many times people look down their nose at us and say, "I've been here on the earth longer than you. What do you know?" Sometimes people despise us because we are not informed enough. St. Paul told Timothy, "Study to show thyself approved unto God, a workman that needeth not to be ashamed, rightly dividing the word of truth" (2 Tim. 2:15). We need to be an informed people, aware of what God is saying in His Word to a dying generation. If we are going to duplicate ourselves, we have to have a high opinion of our God. If we don't have a high opinion of our God, we will be ashamed of the gospel, and of our Savior, and we will not try to duplicate what we are. We'll say, "Well, I'm saved. I'm going to Heaven." But that's not what God told us to do. Jesus is saying, "Get a high opinion of who I am and don't be ashamed of Me. If you are ashamed of Me, I will be ashamed of you before My Father."

It is time to tell people about Him and lead them to Christ and break the yoke. When we stand up on Sunday mornings and do spiritual warfare, we are fighting not only for our immediate families, but also for the people out there who are going to die and go to hell if we don't reach them. There are people next door to us, right down the street from us, who are going to die and go to hell if we don't give them the Word of the Lord.

Walk down the street, knock on the door, and let them know that while they were yet sinners, Christ died for them;

that they were born sinners, but that God has shed His love abroad in our hearts. Let them know that there is a better way than the way they are living. Once we let them know, we have taken the blood off our hands.

Be Confident in Your God-Given Abilities

Take heed to yourself. Don't let anybody despise you. The word *despise* means "regard as beneath one's notice." "She is just one of those holy rollers." "He is one of those religious fanatics."

When Saul saw David for the first time, he said, "Thou art not able to go against this Philistine to fight with him: for thou art but a youth..." (1 Sam. 17:33).

But David did not let Saul look down his nose at him. He responded, "Thy servant kept his father's sheep, and there came a lion, and a bear, and took a lamb out of the flock: And I went out after him, and smote him, and delivered it out of his mouth: and when he arose against me, I caught him by his beard, and smote him, and slew him. Thy servant slew both the lion and the bear..." (1 Sam. 17:34-36). Maybe he was thinking, *How do you know, Saul? You weren't there when I was killing the lion and killing the bear. How do you know what I am able to do?*

Don't let people despise you. They don't know the time you spent in your prayer closet. Nobody saw you when you were on the back side of the mountain down by the burning bush hearing from God. Nobody saw you when you were in the desert of Arabia when God was making, breaking, shaping, and molding you. Nobody saw you on the plains of Bethlehem killing giants, bears, and lions.

Don't be ashamed of your faith, but don't be ashamed to be educated either. It is not wrong to be articulate. It is not wrong to be knowledgeable. Some people think all church people are ignorant anyway. Don't give them a reason to despise you. We can show them that we are not ignorant. We know what time it is. Even Christians who are uneducated know what God is doing in this hour, and that's more important than worldly knowledge. But God also gave us our minds to develop. We need to use and develop what He has given us.

Be Ready to Grow

Statement of truth. It is our responsibility to develop our potential and possibilities with the help of God—to stir our character and our uniqueness. It is our responsibility to cultivate our character. You can be anointed but have a flaw in your character. You can have a position, you can have a place, but be flawed in your character. St. Peter did. He had the revelation of the Christ, the Son of the Living God. He was anointed. He preached.

Jesus said, "Peter, when you are converted, strengthen your brethren."

What do you mean, "converted"? You mean Peter wasn't saved? Yes, Peter was saved. He just had some character flaws that needed to be worked on, even after he became chief apostle. Paul had to stand up to him in Galatia and say to his face, "What are you doing, Peter? You are wrong. You get around the Jews and say one thing and get around the Gentiles and say something else." Peter still had a character flaw. But he had good things about him already, good things that were unique. Peter was always the daring one. He's the one who walked on the water with Jesus.

After Jesus' resurrection, the disciples said, "We are going fishing." They spent the night toiling and working, but caught nothing.

Jesus was standing on the bank, and He said, "Cast your nets on the other side." They had been toiling and laboring all night long in their profession and hadn't caught anything, and somebody came up to them early in the morning and said, "Try the other side. All you have to do is move over a little bit." When they dropped their nets on the other side, they caught fish.

Who was that man on the shore? John said, "It is the Lord." Why didn't anybody else recognize Him? Because John had the closest relationship with Jesus. He was the one who had his head on Jesus' bosom at the Last Supper. When everybody else was running away from the cross and going down to Emmaus, John was there shouting and jumping and dancing and praising the risen Lord. John recognized Him, but it was Peter who put on his coat and jumped into the water. He thought of swimming. Peter had a habit of jumping out of the boat trying to get to Jesus. He left those fish. He left it all to get to Jesus.

When he got ashore, he smelled something. Jesus already had some fish on the grill. Peter sat there and ate the fish with Jesus. Jesus didn't tell Peter, "Feed My lambs; feed My sheep," until after Jesus had fed Peter.

Peter was first. Peter broke out of the mold. He was always willing to go for an adventure.

Stop being afraid. Be willing to go for an adventure and break out of the mold you are in. You know, even when we go witnessing, we go to the houses of people we know. We stay in our comfort zone. Now, the people you know need to be saved, too. But we need to go beyond where we're comfortable.

We need to go into the desert of Arabia as Paul did and develop our potential. Your prayer closet could be your desert. A room in your home could be the back side of the mountain. Your quiet place could be where God deals with you, makes you, molds you, and cultivates you. Listen to God about what you can be. Don't look down on yourself. How do you know what you can't do? You have so much potential. Nobody knows that potential and those possibilities but you. You know your upbringing.

Saul didn't know what David was capable of. Sometimes you have to tell people what you are able to do. You have to say, "Let me tell you something, Saul. I killed a lion and a bear."

Can't you see Saul jump back and say, "What! You smote him?"

"Yes, I smote him and took the lamb out of his mouth. When he came after me, I caught him by his beard."

"You mean you grabbed the lion by his beard?"

"Yeah, I grabbed him by his beard and killed him. I killed the lion and the bear, and I will kill this uncircumcised Philistine, too."

Take heed to yourselves. Tell people what you have done. Tell the world that Jesus has saved you. Tell them what you used to be like, and let them know what you are right now. David knew the capabilities God had blessed him with. You know what God has done in your life. If He has been good to you, you know He's been good. If He has brought you a mighty long way, you know He's brought you. You must not let people despise you when you know God has been good to you.

Some people have overbearing personalities. Have you ever talked with people who just take over the conversation? They want to tell about all the good things the Lord has done for them, but don't want you to get a word in because they are talking to be impressive. We can be intimidated, and shrink back. If we are not careful, they can make our testimony look small. But you need to know "God has done this for me and it is just as big as their testimony. He keeps doing great things for me. Maybe I can't tell my story the way you tell yours, but I know what He has done for me." Somebody may be a better talker than you, but don't be intimidated. Sometimes the quietest folk are the wisest. Just know who you are.

Paul said, "You are apostles, but I'm not behind you. I was just born out of season. I didn't break bread with Him on the night He was betrayed. I wasn't in the garden on that night. But the same thing He gave you on that night, He gave me, too. He took the bread and broke it, and we eat it. He took the cup and blessed it, and we drink it. I wasn't there, but I am still an apostle. Peter is the apostle to the Jews, and I'm the apostle to the Gentiles."

Paul knew who he was, and David knew who he was. They knew because they had been there. But when David killed the lion and the bear, nobody paid David any attention. When Samuel came looking to anoint one of Jesse's sons to be king, did Jesse say, "Oh, you've got to meet David. He killed a lion and a bear"? No, nobody gave David credit.

Have you ever felt like that? Maybe you haven't done anything spectacular. "God," you say, "I didn't kill a lion. I didn't kill a bear. And they overlook me and don't pay any attention to me—none whatsoever. I don't get any credit. Nobody pats me on the back."

When David went into the field and killed the lion, nobody applauded him—nobody but the saints of Heaven, and he couldn't hear that. When he killed the bear, maybe he looked around and asked, "Where is the audience?" There was no audience to applaud him—nothing but the trees and the birds and the sheep and the water.

I dare you to get a personal victory. I dare you to get victory in secret. Then you'll go out in front of the armies of Israel, in front of the Philistines, and kill the giant, and everybody will applaud you. They will applaud the God who has worked through your life. Even the king will have to recognize that God is with you. But you have to get it in private first; then you'll have the confidence when you do it in front of others. Somebody learning to play guitar doesn't stand up and play in public after the first lesson. You practice in private, and when you know you're good, then you do it in public.

Those times when nobody paid David any attention were the times when he was developing his possibilities and cultivating his uniqueness. You need to take advantage of those times when people are overlooking you. Take advantage of those times when people are paying no attention to you. Those are the times to develop your potential and your uniqueness, because there will come a day when those people are going to need you. They will need a warrior to kill Goliath. They will need a Moses to deliver them out of Egypt. They will need a Gideon to fight the Midianites. They will need a Jethro to deliver the people of Israel. If you develop who you are and develop your uniqueness, you will be prepared to fulfill God's purpose for you. The characteristics you are developing will be needed some day, and you will be able to supply the need of the people.

Be an Example

Paul instructed Timothy, "Be thou an example of the believers..." (1 Tim. 4:12). Another translation says, "Be their ideal." In other words, be the believers' model—be their pattern, their standard.

People are going to look at you and you are going to be their ideal. You are going to be their example. They are going to look at you and say, "That's what I need to get." They might not even tell you. But they will look at you and say, "I want to be like that." We affect more lives secretly than openly. So God is telling us to be their pattern, their standard, their ideal, and their model.

Timothy had to be an example in six areas—"in word, in conversation, in charity, in spirit, in faith, in purity."

In word. You need to get some depth in the Word. We learn two Scriptures, then we get a bottle of oil and a briefcase and start a healing ministry—because we know two Scriptures. A half-cocked gun is dangerous. You need to be loaded or unloaded. Be an example in the Word. Be able to search the Scriptures. "Study to show thyself approved unto God, a workman that needeth not to be ashamed, rightly dividing the word of truth" (2 Tim. 2:15). Don't study to show yourself approved unto man. Let God approve you. We need to be the believers' example in the Word.

There's no way I'd go out against nations with just four hundred men. But David, in the cave of Adullam, instructed his men in the Word. These men knew the Word. They knew the law. David had to know it, because many of the things he did, he did in a godly way. He was a loyal man.

In conversation. Conversation means not just the way you talk, but your lifestyle. You have to be an example, a model, a standard, in your lifestyle.

In charity. In love—not *phileo* love, in which I love you because you love me. That's conditional. Not *eros* love. That's erotic love. But *agape* love, in which I love you unconditionally.

In spirit. Let the spirit in which you do things be an example. "I'm doing it because I have to"—that's a nasty spirit. "I'm doing it because the pastor asked me to do it"—that's the wrong spirit. You have to have the right spirit: "I'm doing it because I love God." "Whatsoever ye do in word or deed, do all in the name of the Lord Jesus, giving thanks to God and the Father by Him" (Col. 3:17). Whatever I do, I'm doing it for God, not to be patted on my back. People will overlook things. Even as a pastor, many times I overlook, because I'm human. Sometimes, I will not see your achievement. I will not see your accomplishment. I will not see what you are doing. I will overlook it because I'm doing other things. But if you do it for God and not for man, God will pat you on the back and give you your glory and your reward. God never overlooks anything we do for Him.

In faith. Have unshakable faith. Somebody could say, "I thought I saw the pastor last night at the lounge. Maybe it wasn't him, but I sure thought I saw him." If you are shaky in your faith, when the pastor starts preaching, you will think, "He was at the lounge last night. Now he's up there preaching." Notice, too, the controlling spirit. It puts thoughts in your mind, and then that thought will be controlling you when the Word of God is coming forward. We need to bring every thought into subjection to the knowledge of Christ (see 2 Cor. 10:5). Instead of judging, we need to say, "I know that man of God. If he was at the lounge he had a good reason for being there. Frankly, I don't believe he was at the lounge and maybe this guy saw somebody who looked like him." That's unshakable faith. Have faith in God, and have faith that God has sent you a man of God. If you have sincerely asked God to send you a godly leader, do you think God would send you somebody who would lead you off into error? God is going to give you a man who is sincere, who means business, and who is going to take care of business, and who is going to lead you on to victory. When I was saved, I believed that, and that's what God gave me. I believe that's what God is giving you.

In purity. This is related to your lifestyle, too, and it doesn't just refer to chastity. Everything you do or say should be pure and above reproach. People should be able to see that you are living purely for God.

Practical Advice From Paul

Paul's instructions to Timothy include eight other bits of advice that will bless us if we heed them (see 1 Tim. 4:13-16).

1. "Give attendance to reading." Knowledge is power. Often we are ignorant of things because we don't read. Everybody should read at least one book a week. That's powerful. When I realized I should be doing that as a minister, I repented and said, "O.K." I try to read a book every week. Doing that will increase your vocabulary. It will help you articulate better. It will make you a well-rounded person. You gain knowledge through reading. We all should be knowledgeable. We read the Bible, of course, but many good writers have written *about* the Bible. Get a book and read about the Bible. Have you ever read about the tabernacle? About types and shadows? About the

blood of Jesus? About spiritual warfare? Have you ever read a commentary on Genesis, Exodus, Numbers, Deuteronomy, or Joshua? A commentary on St. Matthew, St. John, St. Luke, St. Mark, or Acts? There are many things written by Holy Ghost-filled writers about the Bible.

2. "Give attendance...to exhortation." Exhortation means pressing and compelling people to action. People need to be exhorted into action and effort. Encourage them to do something. Make them exert effort.

3. "Give attendance...to doctrine." Develop your life in accordance with the teachings of Jesus. "Observe all things whatsoever I have commanded you..." was His final instruction to us (Mt. 28:20).

4. "Neglect not the gift that is in thee." Don't forget it. Don't ignore it. Don't overlook your gift. You can get so caught up in other people's gifts that you forget your own gift. You say, "Their gift is better than my gift." Who told you that? Don't overlook and ignore your gift by trying to get somebody else's. Your gift can be just as powerful if you cultivate it and don't neglect it.

5. "Meditate upon these things." After listening to a sermon or a Sunday school lesson, meditate on it. Do you meditate? I'm not talking about getting into yoga, sitting with your legs crossed, and trying to see into the future. The Lord told Joshua to meditate on the things that are written in the law. Meditate after you read something. Think about it. You will be surprised by how many revelations come. In the morning we might read, "The Lord is my shepherd; I shall not

want," and close the Bible and never meditate on it. "I have to go to work. I got my Scripture reading in for the day." We need to think about it. Whatever is true, honest, just, pure, lovely, of good report; if there be any virtue, and if there be any praise, think on these things (see Phil. 4:8).

6. "Give thyself wholly to them." Let your whole life be guided by your meditation on God and His Word. They will transform your mind. You will begin to do just what you think about. "For as he thinketh in his heart, so is he..." (Prov. 23:7).

7. "Take heed unto thyself." Always take care to be following God's will. Always be taking heed of His Word. Be aware of who you are, and whose you are.

8. "Continue in them." Don't just think about the Word and follow it one day. If you tell somebody about Jesus today, you feel good. Your pastor asks you on Sunday whether you shared the Lord with anyone. "Yeah, I did it Tuesday." What about Wednesday, Thursday, and Friday? Continue.

After Elijah told King Ahab it wasn't going to rain, God told Elijah to hide himself so that God might refresh and feed him. After God refreshes and feeds us, He says, "Go show thyself." Continuing in God's purpose for our lives means going forth in God's will. After we have been refreshed, after we have prepared, after we have succeeded in private, it is time to go forth. People remember what you used to be. Go show them what you are now. People remember what you used to say and what you used to do. Let them see what you say and do now. God tells us, "In showing yourself, I will send rain upon the earth." Somebody is going to be watered by your testimony. Somebody is going to be changed. Those dry and thirsty places and those thirsty and hungry people will be watered by your testimony and by who you are now.

David went out and behaved wisely. If you behave wisely, you mind your P's and Q's. You will be well-founded. You will have a firm foundation. You will be well-favored, pleasing, and delightful. If you behave yourself wisely, God is going to be with you.

Have you ever been around a person who's well-favored, who has a personality that makes you feel good? There was a lady named Rayann who used to work as a ticket agent. I used to enjoy just hearing her explain something, because she had a personality that made you feel good, a personality that was second to none. She was well-conditioned, sound, strong, vigorous, and well-groomed. She manifested care, orderliness, and neatness. She was courteous, mannerly, and polite—a joy to be around.

That's behaving wisely. It will draw people to you. You will become a wellspring, a source, a cause, an origin. You will be well thought of, respectable. God will use your gifts to change people's lives. You will have a great reputation and be a plant of renown. You will show that you are someone with David's spirit upon you and a heart after God.

Chapter 3

Your Gift Will Make Room

Everyone has a particular gift. Before you came out of the womb, God endowed you with special talents and special gifts.

For Thou hast possessed my reins: Thou hast covered me in my mother's womb. ... My substance was not hid from Thee, when I was made in secret, and curiously wrought in the lower parts of the earth. Thine eyes did see my substance, yet being unperfect; and in Thy book all my members were written, which in continuance were fashioned, when as yet there was none of them (Psalm 139:13,15-16).

God was aware of every aspect of our development before birth. Everything about us was written in His book. He knows the talents and abilities and gifts He planted in us. If He calls us to do something, then it's because He knows that the ability is there.

When God called Jeremiah, Jeremiah replied, "Ah, Lord God! behold, I cannot speak: for I am a child" (Jer. 1:6).

But God answered him, "Say not, I am a child: for thou shalt go to all that I shall send thee, and whatsoever I command thee thou shalt speak" (Jer. 1:7).

God told Jeremiah that he had been called to be a prophet even before he was born: "Before I formed thee in the belly I knew thee; and before thou camest forth out of the womb I sanctified thee, and I ordained thee a prophet unto the nations" (Jer. 1:5). If God sanctified and ordained him even before birth, then we know that God endowed him with special gifts to do the job. Whatever it is that God has called you to do, He has endowed you with special gifts to do the job.

You have only one lifetime to be effective for God—one lifetime to make an impact. You can't go back and undo what you did yesterday. If you didn't do anything for the Lord yesterday, you can't go back and do something for Him. You have to look at every day as the day God has allotted you to do something for Him and to bring glory to His name.

We know we have gifts and callings. Even the unsaved have gifts, and God does not take them back. He was there when He made sinners just as He was there when He made you. That is why Scripture says, "Many are called, but few are chosen" (Mt. 22:14). A lot of unsaved people out there have been called to the marriage of the Lamb of God, but we have not yet gotten to them and told them they are invited to the feast.

How will we reach them? God wants to use your particular talents and gifts. Often we find other things to do. But God made you to be you, and you have to take those gifts and talents God has given you and cultivate them and bring them to their fullest potential so that you can have an impact on society. Look at the apostles. Each was unique, each spread the gospel in different ways and to different people, but each apostle was effective. We have to be effective, too.

If God has given you a gift, then He will provide a way for you to use it for His glory. Proverbs 18:16 says, "A man's gift maketh room for him, and bringeth him before great men." Proverbs 17:8 says, "A gift is as a precious stone in the eyes of him that hath it: whithersoever it turneth, it prospereth." If you are gifted—and you are—then your personal gift, your designated talent, will create room for you.

Dependence, Independence, and Interdependence

We have to take responsibility for cultivating that gift and bringing it to the level God desires. That responsibility is yours, and if you cultivate the gift, then the gift will make a place for you. Many times we want be in the company of great people. If you cultivate the gift that God has planted in you, then great people will want to be around you. Bringing the gift to the forefront is not so much telling people, "I have this gift." The gift will speak for itself.

I've heard people say, "I have the gift of prophecy."

Another will say, "I have the gift of healing."

Someone else will say, "I have the gift of working miracles."

If you have the gift of healing, there are many people in the hospital who need you to lay hands on them. Don't just go to church and say, "I have the gift of healing." Somebody out there in the world needs your healing touch. If you have the gift of miracles, people out there in the world need a miracle. Go out there and extend that miracle to them.

Some people say, "I don't like to be around this person because I don't like his personality." That's not an excuse for avoiding people. You have to deal with people the way they are. The Good Samaritan came to the man who was bruised, wounded, and bleeding and he dealt with that man on his level. You have to learn to deal with people on their level. God dealt with you on your level.

In the cave of Adullam, there were four hundred men with different backgrounds, different outlooks on life, different goals, different personalities—four hundred different personalities. I imagine there were some personality clashes in that cave, not to mention some women with their own personalities.

But many times it takes opposites to make things work. This is why your car battery has negative and positive posts. We need somebody with your personality, but we also need people with completely different personalities. We each have unique, individual qualities. Nobody else can be you. Somebody can act like you, or walk like you, or fix himself up to look like you. You see many people fixing themselves up to look like Elvis Presley. They look like him and they try to act like him. They have look-alike contests. They have sing-alike contests. But they are not him, because Elvis Presley had his own unique characteristics. You have your own unique characteristics.

There are three types of people. There are dependent people. There are independent people. And there are interdependent people. A lot of people are dependent. They may be born again, but they still are dependent. If a man is paralyzed, then he is dependent on others to help him around, help him bathe, and help him get dressed. He can be physically paralyzed, yet be mentally and emotionally independent.

Many of God's people are independent physically, but dependent emotionally. Being dependent emotionally means that you put too much value on other people's opinions. If somebody doesn't like you, that can devastate you. If somebody tells you, "I just don't like you and don't want to be around you," that could destroy your day, because you are dependent on that person's opinion of you. You let the other person decide for you who you are.

Some of us are dependent intellectually. We need people to do our thinking for us. We don't like to make decisions even in our own household. If your spouse asks, "What do you think about this?" you tell your spouse to make the decision.

Some of us are dependent financially. We depend on other people's finances to provide for us. In a husband-and-wife team there is nothing wrong with that. The elderly and children are dependent on other people's finances, as are some handicapped adults. But most single people should be self-sufficient financially.

If you are emotionally independent, then nobody will be able to hurt you unless you let them. I can walk up to you and say, "I don't like you." That doesn't have to hurt you. You don't have to let it hurt you. People can say anything they want about you. It's how you receive it that hurts you. If you are dependent emotionally, you are still dependent on people's opinions. "Do they like me?" "Do I sit well with them?" Their opinion defines you. If you are independent emotionally, you will be on the outside who you are on the inside; in your heart, you will know who you are. As long as your self-worth comes from somebody else valuing you, you are a dependent person.

We need to move out of that and stop being dependent emotionally and intellectually. Many of us break out of dependency and into independence. Physical independence means I can dress myself, brush my own teeth, brush my own hair. Becoming emotionally independent means I don't care what anybody thinks about me. My self-worth comes from the inside. I am what I am by the grace of God. I am a tongue-talking, hand-clapping, foot-stomping child of the most high God. My self-worth comes from the inside, which is where the Holy Ghost lives. I am worth something because God said I am worth something, not because people say I am worth something.

Being intellectually independent means I have a mind, I can think and be creative. I am not dependent on others for all my ideas. I can listen to the news or read a book and look at it critically and form my own opinion.

All of this ties into your gift making room for you. When you are independent intellectually, you can think for yourself. You can make decisions for yourself. A lot of people are afraid to make decisions, because they are afraid they are going to make the wrong one. They are afraid of mistakes. When you become afraid of mistakes, it pushes you into a corner so that you are afraid to decide. You are going to be at a standstill and hesitate and do nothing.

To exercise your gift, you have to become independent physically, emotionally, and intellectually, and then you can even move into being independent financially. If you work for somebody else, maybe you can start your own business and set your own hours. But your gift will make room for you.

However, being independent is not the supreme way of doing things. Interdependency is the supreme way.

We break out of a dependent mold, because we don't want to be defined by other people. You don't want them to have you in their little dictionary. When you are dependent, people will define you, manipulate you, control you, and use you. You have to know who you are and who God wants you to be. You have to define that yourself.

When you are independent, you can look at yourself and evaluate what kind of person you are. You can evaluate why you think what you think. Animals can't do that. This is why God gave us dominion. We can stand apart from ourselves and evaluate our own strengths and weaknesses. That is called self-awareness. We can look at ourselves and see whether we are being dependent, independent, or interdependent.

Dependence says, "You let me down. You failed me. You didn't come through for me."

Independence says, "I can do it myself. I can think for myself."

Interdependence says, "We can do it together, you and I." It goes along exactly with the Scriptures. The Scriptures say that two are better than one. If one can chase a thousand, two can put ten thousand to flight. The Scriptures say it's better to have two in bed, because one keeps the other warm. Our Deacon Sheffield says, "One hand must wash the other if you want them clean."

I once built a church in Berkeley, West Virginia—alone. I had to put my block on the scaffold, mix the mortar, throw it up on the scaffold, and lay the block. When I ran out of mortar, I had to get down, and throw some more mortar up. If there had been a laborer there, then instead of building the church in seven months, we could have done it in three and a half, because two can do something quicker than one can, and they can do it better.

But only independent people can become interdependent. You cannot move directly from being dependent to being interdependent. You have to move to independence first. Being interdependent means that I can take my thoughts, my emotions, and my potential, and put them together with your thoughts, emotions, and potential, and we can get something done.

Work Smarter

Many times the people of the Kingdom work hard, but we don't work smart. We have to start working smart.

When we first attended this church, Deacon S. used to cut the grass—a one-man show. Now we have moved up to a four-man show, and they get it cut quicker than one man would. But what if we were working smart, and to those four, we added four more? Instead of cutting the grass in four hours, they could cut it in two. Then everybody could go home and do what they want and nobody would be worn out.

If your gift is going to make room for you, you also must learn to take orders from delegated authority. Suppose the deacons call a work day. Somebody will show up. If the pastor calls a work day, everybody shows up. People need to realize that the pastor has delegated authority to the deacons to call that work day.

We also must value quality. Quality is the degree of excellence—superiority. Suppose you went to the shoe store with $50, and you saw a pair of shoes you wanted for $49.99. The shoes were quality shoes. Then you saw another pair of less quality, and they were $30. I dare say most people would buy the $30 pair because they would still have $20 left. But you would recognize that the more expensive pair had higher quality; they were made better, they would last longer, and in the long run they should be cheaper to own because you wouldn't have to buy another pair so soon.

David pushed for excellence. We should do the same. Whatever you do, you need to do it with a spirit of excellence. You need to put an excellent touch on it. Don't let good become an enemy of better and best. Don't stop and say, "It is good enough." Stop and say, "No, I'm not going to settle for 'good enough.' I'm going to go for the best." Try to do it so that nobody else can top it—not that you are in competition, but that you are doing your very best. God deserves the very best. When God does something, He does His very best. He does it with an excellent touch.

When people ask how I'm doing, I say, "Excellent." I don't care what situation I'm in, I don't care where I am, I don't care how I'm pressed, I don't care what corner I'm backed into, I'm doing excellent. Because in all of that, God is in me. That's why I'm an interdependent person. I am willing to put all my potential and all my abilities with somebody else's and get the job done.

You have to shoot for excellence. You have to shoot for quality. My mother-in-law taught me this. She has an excellent spirit. One time at the store, I watched her buy my children some clothes. She buys the highest-priced clothes. I don't know much about children's clothes, but my wife does, and she pointed out things about the clothes her mother bought. She said to me, "You see this here?"

"Yeah," I said. "Looks like clothes to me."

But she went on to explain what made them quality clothes. That is the way my mother-in-law is. She buys herself the most expensive stuff, and there is nothing wrong with that. It is just having a spirit of excellence. She is using her money wisely to get things of quality that will last.

Have a spirit of excellence, because after you leave church you become a role model out in your community. Are people going to look at you and say, "That's what I want to be"? You teach not just by words, but by example. If we're going to teach people something by example, we have to be quality individuals. We have to shoot for excellence.

Statement of truth. There are qualities in our life that God Himself has built into us, because we are called by God, chosen ones, according to His purpose. These qualities cause us to excel, to achieve, and to progress.

Duplicate God's Heart

One of the theme Scriptures of my life is Psalm 78:72. "He fed them according to the integrity of His heart; and guided them by the skilfulness of His hands." The Scripture is talking about God, but David is mentioned too. David was a holy person, and what David was on the inside showed up on the outside.

Yet, David had two sides. On the one side, he was a murderer, an adulterer, and a liar. On the other side, David was a man after God's own heart. Why did God keep David around when He threw Saul away? Saul sinned and God tossed him away. David sinned and God forgave him. What was the difference? David had a heart patterned after God's own. It is hard for God to throw away His own heart. Saul didn't have that.

God loves loving-kindness; God loves mercy; God's love is wrapped up in His being. David had that type of heart, so God couldn't kill him or throw him away. God had to forgive him, because David was sorry for what he'd done, and he kept running after God. He had a duplicate of God's heart.

God wants us to have duplicates of His heart, and to keep making more copies. The world does it every day. There's a McDonald's over on highway 90. When I drive further down along the beach there's another McDonald's. I keep going and I see a McDonald's along Pass Road, and a McDonald's on 49. In almost any city you can find a McDonald's. McDonald's keeps duplicating itself.

The same with Hancock Banks. Hancock Banks just bought People's Federal. And they just keep duplicating themselves. They bought a bank in Waveland and are going to make it a Hancock Bank. They bought one in Diamondhead and are going to make it a Hancock Bank. They keep duplicating. They have a pattern.

This is what God does. He gets a man and He duplicates Him. That man is Christ Jesus.

Gifts and Callings Are for Life

Romans 11:29 says, "The gifts and calling of God are without repentance." If God has given you a gift or a calling, He's not going to take it away. The Greek word for gift is *charisma*. In English, this word speaks of charm or ability. This word is also closely related to *charismatic*, which refers to people who place much emphasis on the gifts of the Spirit. The Greek root behind charisma is *charos*, which means "grace," signifying that God gives gifts, abilities, and talents to individuals because of His grace, not as a reward for our goodness.

In everyone's life, there is some kind of charisma. You have ability. Not only do you have ability, you have charm. You can charm people in your own way. That's why just about every man can get a wife. And every woman can get a husband. Each person has some kind of charm that is attractive to somebody else.

You say that a man or woman has charmed you. They know just what to say, and how to say it. Even on the natural side, you have charisma, which enables you to get a job. There is something built into your character. You can do a specific job in a specific way for the boss.

So the word *gift* means "charisma," and it is related to the gifts of the Spirit. Not only does God give us ability, but our abilities work by the administration of the Holy Ghost. Some gifts are entirely God working through us. If I have the gift of healing, then why do I sometimes lay hands on somebody and nothing happens? Because it's not so much that we have a gift, as it is the Holy Ghost administering it. If the gift were mine, I could heal everybody. But He gives us the grace, and it doesn't operate when we want it to operate. It operates when He wants it to operate. So I lay hands on people and sometimes they are not healed. Sometimes, I lay hands on people and they are instantly healed. I can't heal a flea. Somebody said I can't heal a bald-headed bumble bee. I can't. But when we lay hands on the sick in the name of the Lord Jesus Christ, when the Holy Ghost administers that gift through us, anybody can be healed.

Sometimes, I come into the service and the spirit of prophecy is upon me, and everybody gets a word. At other times, nobody gets anything except what I am preaching. That's when your personal word comes forward. So God gives us the grace according to His timing. He uses our talents and gifts at the time of His choosing.

Eli was high priest of Israel. Although Eli did not do right with his sons—he allowed the ark of glory to be taken out to battle by a sinful man—he still died as high priest of Israel. God called him and gave him that position, and Eli died in that same position.

Look at Saul. God chose this man, then rejected him because of his disobedience. But even after God rejected him, Saul reigned in Israel for a number of years. When he died, he was still king of Israel. God had already anointed somebody else. Basically, Saul had already been fired. He had lost the anointing. David could have killed him, but David said, "I won't touch God's anointed." That's loyalty. When Saul died on the battlefield, he still had the crown on his head. God didn't strip him down and take away the kingship and send him off to die as a pauper or as a servant.

If God ever places you in something, if God ever calls you to be something, you can assure yourself that you are going to die as whatever He called you to be.

Look at Judas. He betrayed Jesus and sold Him for a few pieces of silver. Even on the night Judas betrayed Him, when Judas brought the high priest and others into the garden, Jesus called him "My friend." When Judas died, he was still a disciple, just a backslidden one.

If I were to backslide today and die, they wouldn't just say, "Jeffrey Reed died." They would say, "Reverend Reed died." If I were to backslide and open up a barroom, God forbid, and never come to the church again, when I died they would still call me "Reverend," because gifts and callings are for life. Once God calls you and gives you a gift, you will die with that gift, whether you are using it or not.

There are a lot of backslidden preachers in pulpits. Jeremiah said God spoke to him and said, "I didn't send them. They just went. I tell them to say nothing. They just speak out of their own hearts." A lot of people are following some of the backslidden preachers, even though these preachers have been fired. God hasn't taken away His calling for them to be holy preachers, but He has temporarily revoked their license to preach.

This applies not only to backslidden pastors. There are people in leadership positions who can't handle the positions. God has rejected them. They are twice dead. God is just waiting for you to come out of Adullam. God is raising up people to spread the gospel for Him. He is training you in the cave of Adullam, and He is going to send you forth out of the cave. God is just waiting for you to walk out of Adullam as a giant-slayer.

Long after Saul had been fired, God was just waiting for David. David inherited the throne when Samuel anointed him. But first God had to work some things out in his life. With many people, God is just working things out in their lives. But they have inherited their throne already.

Cultivate Your Gift

Paul urged Timothy, "Neglect not the gift that is in thee" (1 Tim. 4:14). Another meaning is "Develop the gift that is in thee." To develop our gift means to express it more fully and in greater detail—to expand it; to amplify it; to enlarge it. When David took the throne, the Bible says, his kingdom was enlarged. His kingdom expanded. The tribe of Levi came under him, along with the tribes of Issachar, Simeon, and Benjamin. If we know in what area we are called, where we are gifted, we can enlarge on that area.

As an interdependent person, you can think your own thoughts. Your success does not depend on what others think about you. Many times we as a people stand still. There is no more growth. There is no more progress. We reach certain peaks and say we can level out, or we are topped out.

You don't level out in God's Kingdom. In God's Kingdom you do not climb and then reach a plateau. God's Kingdom is progress, all the way through life. It is our responsibility to develop our gift, to express it more fully and in greater detail, to expand it, to amplify it, and to enlarge it.

My wife started piano lessons this week. She really is trying to expand her ability. People told her, "You already play well. You already direct the musicians well." But she is not satisfied.

I try to read a book a week. I may be a good teacher and preacher, but I'm not satisfied. I'm not content. I want to expand and amplify. I want to enlarge. I want to be better tomorrow.

We are where we are today because of choices we made yesterday.

Be Responsible

Many times we have complaints against people and find fault with people when the problem is not really the people—it is us. We let what they say affect us. That makes us reactive. There are responsible people, and there are reactive people. Responsible people have response-ability—the ability to choose their response.

Jesus said, "Love your enemy." My enemy, just by the very fact that he is my enemy, makes me want to hate him. But Jesus said to love him, because we have the ability to choose the way we respond. If somebody smites you on the cheek, you have the ability to choose your response. Jesus said the response should be to turn the other one. That's what a responsible person can do.

But many people in God's Kingdom are not responsible. They don't have the ability to respond in the correct way. If somebody doesn't want to be bothered with them, they say, "I don't want to be bothered with you either." They choose to respond that way, which is not following Kingdom principles. If somebody says, "You are not a nice person," they say, "You're not so nice yourself." They could have chosen another response: "I'm sorry you feel that way about me, but I think you are a pretty nice person, a sweet person."

A reactive person sees it's cloudy outside. It might start raining. Reactive people decide they're going to have a bad day. The weather determines how they feel. Responsible people carry their weather with them. They don't care whether it's raining or the sun is shining.

People have a social climate, a social weather. A responsible person says, "I don't care what people think about me because I am what I am; I have self-value and self-worth. I'm a person of integrity. You might treat me wrong, but I'm going to treat you fair, because it is not in my character to treat you the way you treat me. It's not even in my makeup to get back at you."

A reactive person says, "I'm going to talk about you. I'm going to backstab you." A reactive person will bow to the weaknesses of others. The weaknesses of other people control a reactive person's life. You can be under the control of other people and not even know it.

I heard that the Queen of England was walking down the sidewalk and a dog kept barking and barking, and she kept on walking. Somebody asked, "Aren't you going to tell the dog something?"

"No. I'm the Queen of England. I'm not going to bark back at the dog."

Statement of truth. With the help of God, there are levels we can attain. I would compare it to levels in football. There is the peewee league. There is the junior high level. There is the high school level. There is the college level. There is the professional level. The professional level is like the highest calling of God.

Some of us stay in the peewee league all our life. We never mature enough to risk getting hurt. Somebody touches us a little bit and we start crying.

Some move on to the junior high level but never progress further. We don't want to be bothered with people.

Some move up to the high school level and quit there. We are adolescents in the Kingdom.

Some get to the college level and then give up. They have learned a lot but are not fully mature.

I dare you to make it to the professional level. Paul said, "I press for the high calling of God that is in Christ Jesus."

Use Your Gift

In Second Timothy 1:6, we are commanded, "Stir up the gift of God, which is in thee by the putting on of my hands." Another meaning for "stir up" is "fire up." Fire up the gift of God that is in you. *Stir* means "arouse." How many of your gifts are sleeping? On vacation? You need to wake them up; put them to work. Feed the fire. The gifts we have will make room for us.

A friend of mine recently told me that if I came to his convention, he would make space in his program or create an opening so that I could speak to the people. The gifts that lie inside you open doors for you; they cause provision to happen.

Our gift brings us before great men.

Statement of truth. Often, the way we arrive at greatness or before great men is by riding on the gifts with which God has endowed us.

"Every good gift and every perfect gift is from above, and cometh down from the Father of lights..." (Jas. 1:17). Jesus said that when He would ascend into Heaven, He would send gifts to men.

It was the Lord who gave Joseph ability and favor in the sight of the jailer (Gen. 39:21). The gift that was in him made a way for him. He was talented, a gifted administrator. His gift brought him before Pharaoh.

It was the Lord who gave the Israelites ability and favor in the sight of the Egyptians at the time of their exodus (Ex. 3:21).

God gave Esther favor in the sight of King Ahasuerus (Esther 5:2).

God gave Daniel and his friends ability and favor in the sight of the Babylonians (Dan. 1:15-17).

God gave His Son so that we might have the ability not to destroy ourselves but to save ourselves from this untoward generation (Jn. 3:16).

We have the same ability and the same gifts they had. Let's count our gifts as precious stones, and let God ever administer those gifts through us and let those gifts prosper. Once we have done that, our ministry will be more effective in bringing glory to the Kingdom of God.

Chapter 4

The Fivefold Ministry

*A*nd He gave some, apostles; and some, prophets; and
some, evangelists; and some, pastors and teachers; For
the perfecting of the saints, for the work of ministry,
for the edifying of the body of Christ* (Ephesians 4:11-12).

Apostles are those builders, those burden bearers, who
go in there and get the job done. They can bring something
out of nothing. They are represented by the ox that Ezekiel
saw on the cherubim that had four faces. The apostle can
bear the burden in the heat of the day. He doesn't even
know the word *quit*. He doesn't know what *give up* means.
He can toil and work until something happens. Jesus knew
what He was doing when He said to Peter, "Follow Me."

The apostles toiled all night long and caught nothing.
But they toiled. Many fishermen would have given up after
an hour. The wind was too strong. The water was too low.
The water was too wet—any kind of excuse to throw in the
towel. But on several occasions, they toiled all night long and

caught nothing. An apostle will hang in there. Sometimes it means toiling until Jesus comes. When Jesus shows up, He will tell you where the fish are. "Just let your net down on the other side." Apostles will do it. Apostles are the ones sent by God.

Prophets are the seers. They see. They tell people what God is doing, and what He's going to do.

Evangelists have the gift of exhortation. They can light your fire. They can rekindle the flame that is about to die.

Pastors and **teachers** are among the most important. The pastor has to be there with you. He has to counsel you. He has to teach you. He has to lead you. He is the one who sends out the apostle. He sends out the prophet. He makes the evangelist. He makes the teachers. He makes other pastors.

These five offices are called the fivefold ministry—fivefold, just like the five fingers on your hand. If you cut off any one of these fingers, your hand is not capable of performing 100 percent. If you cut out any one of these ministries, you are cutting out a vital part of the Body of Christ.

We need every one of the five gifts: apostles, prophets, evangelists, pastors, and teachers. We have all of them, but many people and many organizations cut out the prophets and the apostles, and say they are not for today. That's a lie from the pit of hell. It's a lie designed to make the Body of Christ ineffective. If there are no prophets, then you have nobody seeing what God wants done. The Body goes blind. If there are no apostles, then you have nobody who will hang in there and toil until something materializes. People today want something ready made. They don't want to work and bring something out of nothing.

But God has other ideas. The apostles are still here. The prophets are still here; they are still saying, "Thus saith the Lord." These ministerial gifts were given when Christ ascended into Heaven. I call them the ascension gifts because of when they were given, and because these are the gifts that ascend, that reach to Heaven.

I'm used in an ascension gift when I'm teaching. I'm also in the office of teacher. There is a difference. There is a difference between pastoring and having the office of pastor, between prophesying and having the office of prophet.

I not only prophesy, but I hold the office of prophet. When you hold the office of prophet, what you say is the law. In the Old Testament, God didn't even have to say it first. If the prophet said it, God would back it up. In the New Testament, Paul would say, "I say this—not the Lord, but I say it." God backed him up: his words are recorded in the Holy Scriptures. But not everybody who prophesies is a prophet.

There is the office of apostle, the sent one. But not everybody who is sent is an apostle.

For the Perfecting of the Saints

These ascension gifts are offices that God gave to the Church for the perfecting of the saints. These offices, these ascension gifts, perfect you.

You won't be made perfect unless you get to a place where these gifts can be found. If you stay home, if you don't reach out and get to where these gifts are operating, then you will never be as effective as you can be in the Body of Christ.

In the Old Testament, we see that people made their way to the prophets. Elisha prophesied that the woman would have a son, and God gave her a son. When the son died, she didn't wait for the prophet to come back. She told her servant to saddle up the donkey. "Ride quickly. We have to find the prophet; he gave us the son, so he has to raise the son from the dead." She went looking for the man of God.

Our situation today is no different. We need to go where the man of God is. Forsake not "the assembling of ourselves together" as you see the day of the Lord approaching. Some people go to church only on Sunday, and then only for an hour. I don't understand it. If I'm looking to become complete, to be perfected, I want to go hear what God is saying. And I know that every time the church doors are open, the Lord is going to meet us there. Almighty God—the One who sits high and looks low; the One whom the universe cannot contain; the alpha and omega; the One who is omnipresent, omnipotent, and omniscient; the great God—bows down and stoops so low as to come visit His Body and speaks to us, and we say, "I'm tired."

The awesome God who doesn't even need us, the One who created the world out of nothing, the One who was pregnant with everything, comes to speak to us, and we say, "I have to work tomorrow."

You can't get it if you don't come. There's nothing like hearing it firsthand from God. Other people can tell us about it, but we won't fully get the message. Some of us from my congregation went to New Orleans to hear Myles Munroe. When I got back, I couldn't tell his message right. You just had to be there.

If you love God, you will want to be there. David said, "I was glad when they said unto me, Let us go into the house of the Lord" (Ps. 122:1). David knew that once he got into the house of the Lord, one of the gifts would kick in, and he would take another step toward perfection. Although he was king, David needed a prophet, and he had a prophet. Even a king needs to be perfected.

For the Work of Ministry

Why are we being perfected through the fivefold ministry? For the work of ministry. The graces we receive are given to us so that we might bless others. God wants His life in us to overflow and reach out to others. Somebody else needs what we have been given in the house of the Lord. There is work to be performed.

We have to reach the point where we don't compromise. When we are in the midst of sinners, we cannot be ashamed of the gospel of Christ. We have to tell them the good news. That's the work of the ministry. Teaching is work. Recalling what God has said, then breaking the bread of life and giving it to somebody else—that's work.

Sometimes we're afraid that people will think we're religious fanatics. That's because they have a mistaken idea of religion. They get that idea from people who "seem to be religious" but who don't bridle their tongues, and who deceive their own hearts (see Jas. 1:26). "Pure religion and undefiled before God and the Father is this, To visit the fatherless and widows in their affliction, and to keep himself unspotted from the world" (Jas. 1:27). People who practice pure religion don't get labeled "religious fanatics." We have to follow the advice of John: "Let us not love in word, neither in tongue; but in deed and in truth" (1 Jn. 3:18). A religious fanatic is somebody who talks about God but doesn't live God.

We should be ambassadors for Christ. People will learn about Christ from us—from hearing what we say, and by comparing our words with our actions. If we talk about God but don't live God, they are not going to find out who Christ is. We show God's love to others because that is His nature, which He shares with us. We're not showing love in order to get people's approval.

Our Mission

We're on a mission in a foreign land. Don't get too attached to this world, because this is not your home. You are an ambassador here on earth. No wonder Abraham said, "I'm a pilgrim and a stranger in this land." He looked for a city whose builder and maker is God. Many times we get so attached to earthly things that we are afraid to tell anybody anything about Christ. We are afraid of what they are going to think about us. We must not be afraid. We are here representing our king, and we have a job to do before He comes back.

Sometimes we don't do our job. We act like there is nothing beyond our present existence. We try to keep up with the Joneses. We try to do what everybody else is doing. That is not our mission. Our mission is to do the right thing effectively.

To be effective and to be a leader, you can't do your work in a corner. You have to tell somebody. You have to reach out and bring people to Christ. We need to be not just leaders, but effective leaders. You can be a leader and be a wrong leader. I am a rabbit hunter; I have dogs, and I have a lead dog. Every pack of dogs has a lead dog. If that lead dog goes up a trail the wrong way, he is likely to get shot in the woods and left there dead. As the leader, he would be not only going the wrong way, he would be messing up everything else. If you are going to lead, you must be effective. If that lead dog barks, all the other dogs in the pack know he is right. He'd better be right, or he won't be around long.

If you are an effective leader, when you speak, everybody will shut up and listen. God puts the word in your mouth as fire and makes the people roar.

The fivefold ministry perfects you, but you have to work it out. You have to reach people. You have to go to the hospitals, to the rest homes, to the street corners. You have to reach out and bring people in. That is not the job of the pastor. That is not the job of the apostle or the prophet. Their job is to perfect *you* to do the work of the ministry.

Jesus perfected the apostles and sent them out two by two. Seventy-two came back rejoicing, saying, "Lord, even the devils obey us."

"Don't rejoice because the devils are subject to you," Jesus said. "Rejoice because your names are written in the Book of Life." If you go out and work in ministry, you will feel satisfied. You will feel fulfilled. Many people get frustrated and oppressed, depressed and all other kinds of "pressed," because they are not doing the thing that God has put inside them. When you are acting in the purpose God has for you, you will be content.

For the Edifying of the Body of Christ

Not only do we have to reach out to a dying world, we have to exhort one another; we have to encourage one another. This means not only that leaders must encourage the people under them, but that people must also encourage their leaders.

When Joshua took over as leader of Israel, the people said to him:

All that thou commandest us we will do, and whithersoever thou sendest us, we will go. According as we hearkened unto Moses in all things, so will we hearken unto thee: only the Lord thy God be with thee, as He was with Moses. Whosoever he be that doth rebel against thy commandment, and will not hearken unto thy words in all that thou commandest him, he shall be put to death: only be strong and of a good courage (Joshua 1:16-18).

Notice what they said: All that you command us, we will do. Wherever you send us, we will go. As we listened to Moses in all things, we will listen to you.

How does this work out in a church congregation? I have ministers and leaders under me. They can disagree with what I say and what I do, and that is all right. But if they begin to spread disagreement through the congregation, God is going to do get rid of them quickly, because the word of the King is law.

When I was under a pastor, there were things he said I didn't agree with. I didn't go to the congregation and say, "That's not right," because God hates discord. If someone sows discord among the brethren, He hates it. He gets rid of them. If my pastor said something I didn't agree with, I went to him and said, "I don't agree with that. Could you explain that to me further and give me some understanding of what you are saying?"

I went to the pastor one time and he told me, "That is just the way it is. That is just what I said."

"O.K. That didn't give me any clarity on it, but if that's what you said, that's what you said." After that, I said nothing more about the matter. I didn't go throughout the congregation saying, "I don't agree with that," or "Don't you let that get into your spirit." That would be sowing discord.

If you don't agree with something your pastor says, the right thing to do is to go to the one who said it. Don't ask his neighbor. Go to him.

Effective Leadership

When both the people and their leaders do their part, it promotes victory. It makes for effective leadership.

Effective means "producing a desired result," "adequate," "capable," "able," "sound," "dynamic." That is what we want to be as leaders, whether we are a leader in a church, or a leader in a home, or leading others by example. We want to produce a desired result. We want to be capable, sound, and dynamic.

People want somebody who is capable, somebody who can get the job done, whatever the job may be. You will be effective if somebody teaching you can also learn from you. Somebody planting the Word of God in your life will also have the Word of God planted by you. It doesn't matter if others have titles in front of their name. Titles don't mean anything. It's a relationship with God that matters. Maybe somebody else got saved before you did, but you may have passed them in spiritual maturity.

Remember the goose that laid golden eggs? You take care of the goose and she will take care of you. You have to know what to do with the goose, and you have to know what to do with the golden eggs. The farmer who got greedy was ineffective, and pretty soon he didn't have the goose or the golden eggs. An effective farmer would say, "I'm going to feed the goose and she's going to give me the eggs. And I'm going to do right with the eggs, so that I can keep on feeding the goose. When she gives me a golden egg, I'm going to buy some feed for the goose and use the rest for myself. But I'm going to make sure the goose is taken care of."

You have to take care of the thing that is producing results. When you are producing results, God will take care of you. It takes time, and you need His care to develop and mature. He will care for you, and He will preserve you until your work is accomplished. God never started anything He wasn't going to finish. He will crown your efforts with success.

Search for Effective Leaders

"There are many devices in a man's heart; nevertheless the counsel of the Lord, that shall stand" (Prov. 19:21). The purpose of God will stand. God is going to take us someplace, because He put us here to go to that destination. Disagreements come along the way. We sway and we rock and we roll. We are influenced by other people who mean us no good and divert us from our destination. You need to keep your eyes on where God is taking you, and look for effective leaders who will guide you there. Effective leaders can see where people are going. They see what God wants.

Many people are trying to become popular and famous. God doesn't care about fame and popularity. God can't use you if you are trying to become famous or popular. God just wants us to be right and to do the right thing, to see what He wants, and to work toward being that.

Sometimes I see my ministry appearing to dwindle; then I see it picking up. I go on just the same. God is in control; God is in charge. If I see a falling away, I say, "God, you are right on target, because You said that in the last days they will fall away." Then I see a sprouting up, a springing forward, and new life coming in. But I keep on preaching and teaching as I have always done. I haven't changed.

Stay With God

Sometimes you'll see newlyweds, the man in the driver's seat and the woman sitting right next to him. Five years pass, and the woman is over against the door. The man didn't move; the woman did.

That is the way it is with God. He is behind the wheel. He has a destination. He's going somewhere, either with you or without you. If you open the car door and jump out, He is still driving. He is still on the way to the destination.

At times, the Church has moved away from her Husband. She has to move back next to Him and stick with Him, no matter how many bumps there are in the road.

Individual churches need to stay beside their pastor, no matter how many potholes he hits, no matter how many times he almost wrecks the car, no matter how many people pull out in front of him. He is still in the driver's seat.

Effective leaders have people who stay glued to their source and see where the leader is going and what he is doing. Yes, there are going to be some potholes. There are going to be some mountains to climb. But if you have an effective leader, then you have some horsepower under the hood; you have enough power to take you up any mountain. There is enough horsepower to take you through any valley, through the rain, through the snows of life. But you have to stick with the driver in order to arrive at the destination.

Stick with leaders who are going where you want to go. But remember that, in reality, you aren't just a passenger. The pastor is taking you somewhere to do the work of ministry. It will be up to you to be effective. "Obey them that have the rule over you, and submit yourselves: for they watch for your souls, as they that must give account, that they may do it with joy…" (Heb. 13:17). In the end, the pastor can either give a joyful report of you or a report that is not so joyful.

The pastor's job is to perfect you. By doing that, he is earning a reward, a pastor's crown. What will you do with the perfection that God works in you?

Leaders Are a Gift

God is always giving out gifts. Many people abuse pastors, because they don't realize that their pastors are gifts. When you don't understand the purpose of a thing, you are likely to abuse it. When you don't understand that your pastor is a gift, you talk negatively. You tell him what you aren't going to do. You tell him where you aren't going to go. That's not what the people told Joshua. They discerned that he was a gift from God. They wanted to get to Canaan, a land flowing with milk and honey. To get there, they needed to stick with the man who would take them.

You can act religious but not be saved. You can belong to a church, have your name on the roll, but not be born again. You won't know where you are going. You won't know the purpose of your spouse, your pastor, or the people around you. If you knew their purpose, you wouldn't treat them the way you do.

Not only is the fivefold ministry a gift to you, but also ministers are a gift, deacons are a gift, missionaries are a gift, musicians are a gift, and ushers are a gift. They are gifts for the perfecting of the saints. They are given to equip you, to polish you, to give you an elegant finish, to improve you, to mend you, and to mature you. You are not yet all that you are supposed to be.

Potential

You are a seed. A seed is a potential tree. From that tree could come hundreds or thousands more. So a seed is a potential forest. You have potential in you that you don't even know about.

One of the greatest threats to your potential is success. I can stop right where I am and say, "I'm already successful." I have a church, a house, a car, a wife who loves me, and children who love me. Success becomes my enemy, because potential is not what you see. Potential is what you don't see. Potential is not what I've done. Potential is what I can do. All you see is the tree. You haven't seen the forest, yet.

We sometimes let success stop us. When you have accomplished all that you want to accomplish, then you have reached a plateau of effectiveness. God can take you off the scene. But if you say, "I have done this, now I can do that," God can keep using you. No wonder Moses stayed around until he was 120. At age 40, in Pharaoh's court, he might have thought he'd done everything he could. When he was 80 years old, with a wife and a family, he might have thought, "I'm successful."

God spoke to him and said, "Now you are really getting ready to step into your fullest potential. Go to Pharaoh and say, 'Let my people go.' "

"I can't. I'm eighty years old. I can't speak."

"I'm God. Didn't I make the tongue?"

Moses still had a lot more to do.

Tragedy is when the tree dies in the seed. Nobody knows what it could have been.

Tragedy is in the graveyard, too, even though it is one of the richest places on earth. It holds inventions you ought to be enjoying right now; they died in the mind of someone. It holds cures for your body, songs you ought to be singing, and books you could be reading. The graveyard holds potential that was never realized. Don't let your potential end up there.

You pastor is a gift to you, to make sure you don't stop growing. Growth takes rebukes and compliments. Nobody likes rebukes. But whether he has to do it through rebukes, compliments, counseling, teaching, or preaching, he does it so that you can be what God expects you to be. God gives us leaders who are vigorous, fearless, and persistent to build up the Body of Christ, to maximize its potential.

The Hidden Work of Ministry

Ministry involves a tremendous amount of work. Some work is open and evident, but much of the work is unseen. Some people don't want to do anything that's not in the limelight where others can see them. Jesus will tell them, "Don't look for a crown. You have your reward already." When you are working in ministry, don't look for people to see you. Work for them to see Jesus.

If you went into the bathrooms at our church, you'll find that they are clean and smell nice. You wouldn't know who cleaned them, but you wouldn't have to see them, because somebody did it for the Lord. If you came into the church, you would find the chairs nice and straight, and the floor clean. Outside, the grass is cut. A lot of the work is unseen. A lot of the work is not in the limelight.

The day is going to come when I will build a fence around my yard and put some Rottweilers in there. Then, when someone wants to see the pastor, they will have to call first. Some people don't realize that there are servants in my church besides me.

Jethro told Moses: "Get some men and appoint them over thousands, over hundreds, and over tens, and let them deal with problems. If you don't, you are going to wear yourself out. You are trying to handle all this, and you don't even have time to spend with your family. You are working from sunup to sundown, and still you are not finished." (See Exodus 18:21-22.)

Moses couldn't do it all. No pastor can.

Proverbs 14:28 says, "In the multitude of people is the king's honour...." The multitude of people serving in ministry bring honor to the church leaders. Leaders do not face an easy task. God has given them an assignment that can be accomplished only through divine intervention or by their own persistence. It means continuing in a course of action without regard to discouragement, opposition, or previous failure. It is their people, including all the unseen workers, who bring them honor, who make the fivefold ministry bear fruit.

However, a leader must also beware of the Absaloms in his congregation, who desire to bring down the Kingdom rather than edify it. Where there are those who only desire to bring honor to their leader, there are also those who would encourage rebellion.

Chapter 5

Beware of Absalom

When things get tough, the weak get going. They take off. They desert you when you need help the most.

It was going on in New Testament times.

Jesus said unto them, Verily, verily, I say unto you, Except ye eat the flesh of the Son of man, and drink His blood, ye have no life in you. Whoso eateth My flesh, and drinketh My blood, hath eternal life; and I will raise him up at the last day. For My flesh is meat indeed, and My blood is drink indeed. He that eateth My flesh, and drinketh My blood, dwelleth in Me, and I in him. As the living Father hath sent Me, and I live by the Father: so he that eateth Me, even he shall live by Me. ... Many therefore of His disciples, when they heard this, said, This is an hard saying; who can hear it? ...From that time many of His disciples went back, and walked no more with Him (John 6:53-57,60,66).

It was going on in Old Testament times, too.

Korah and his cronies "gathered themselves together against Moses and against Aaron..." (Num. 16:3). Moses was the anointed leader of Israel. Korah was a prophet. Korah said to Moses, "You and Aaron are not the only ones God speaks to. We are holy men just like you."

"I don't disagree with you. You are priests. You are worshipping God," Moses said.

"Yeah, but you act like you are it."

Moses said, "I am it. God might speak to you, but He doesn't speak to you the way He speaks to me. I'm the one God put in charge. Tomorrow, Korah, we'll see who God chooses."

By the next day, Korah had built his army up to 250 men, resisting the authority God had established. The earth opened up, swallowed them, and burned them up.

People sometimes confuse meekness with weakness. Moses was meek, but meekness is strength. Moses was strong, but he wasn't a bully.

The people had the nerve to turn around and say to Moses, "You killed Korah."

God said, "Listen to those people!" He went through the camp and a plague broke out.

"Aaron," Moses said, "a plague has broken out in the camp. Get your censer." Aaron took his censer and ran out to the middle of the camp. That's where the plague stopped.

Korah wasn't the first among the Israelites to rebel. Miriam, Moses' sister, rebelled in criticizing Moses' wife. Miriam was smitten with leprosy, and God said, "Listen. This is My man. This is the one I have ordained."

Then He said to Moses, "Set her outside the camp for seven days."

Moses prayed, "God, spare my sister." Moses, the very one against whom she had incited rebellion, was the one she needed to heal her.

How Far Will We Follow?

Jesus said, "Unless you eat My flesh and drink My blood, you have no life in you." That seems gross, doesn't it? It does if you don't know and understand Jesus. You have to understand the condition of this world—it's the same today as it was in Jesus' time. Many people have had a religious experience, and because of that they think they know Jesus.

The Bible says, "Follow on to know the Lord..." (Hos. 6:3). Sometimes people hear or feel the Spirit of God tug them. They feel the touch of the Holy Spirit, but they try to freeze it. They build a tradition out of their limited experience of God. Tradition can freeze experience.

Jesus said, "Away with your traditions, because you have made the commandments of God to none effect" (see Mt. 15:6). We have to follow on. When He multiplied fish and bread to feed the multitude, the crowd was ready to follow Him as long as they would get more of the same. They weren't ready to go any further spiritually. Jesus saw the multitude following Him, and He knew that in their hearts they meant Him no good. They were interested only in what they could get out of Him.

He was inviting them to make a commitment to who He was. But His Kingdom is not of this world. The multitude didn't understand His Kingdom; they were following Him to get a free lunch, and hoping He might overthrow the

Roman government. Their minds were wrapped up in the system of this world.

Our thinking and mentality have to be completely changed around. We are born under the system of this world, but we need to learn the system of God. Many times we are too comfortable with the world's system and don't want to change to God's way of doing things. But the more I learn about the Bible, and the more I see of the system of the world, the more I disagree with the world's way of doing things.

I read in *Money* magazine about the top one hundred charities ranked by to how much money they raise. I didn't see the Church in there. I did see a gay group that had raised $14.3 million. I saw Ducks Unlimited, but no efforts to stop abortion. You see how backwards the world's system is? We save ducks and kill babies.

Stay With Jesus

A relationship with God isn't measured by whether you have your name on a church roll. Having a position in the church or being active in the church isn't the same as knowing God. Scrap the idea that being a church member is the same as being saved. Working in a church does not give you a relationship with God. You have to be born again to enter the Kingdom of God.

Because you've had a religious experience, your pastor might give you a position when you've not even been born again. That's doing it backwards. Where the Church has gotten backwards, it needs to get turned around and put Jesus first. The real Church says you have to eat His flesh and drink His blood. Then let Him anoint you.

You can worship Him with your lips and yet be far from Him in your heart. Being born again involves a heart transformation. In God's Kingdom everyone has a heart of flesh replacing the old, stony heart, and everyone knows the Lord.

The Jews understood the significance of knowing the Lord. *Knowledge* signified an intimate relationship. It meant being intertwined. St. Paul wrote that carnal knowledge binds you to your sexual partner. A man who joins himself to a harlot becomes one with her. Knowing God means being permanently united to Him.

Unity in Blood Covenants

We read in Genesis that when God made a covenant with Abraham, Abraham took a bullock, cut it in half, and spread it out. He fell into a deep sleep and God walked between the halves of the bullock. In the Old Testament, when men made a covenant, they would cut an animal in half, spill the blood, and walk between the halves, signifying: If one of us should break this covenant, let the same thing happen to him that happened to this animal—let him die. The blood of the animal sealed the covenant.

Divorce is the breaking of a blood covenant. The consummation of the marriage covenant involves the shedding of blood. When a woman's hymen is broken the first time she has intercourse, the shedding of blood seals the relationship. *Hymen* in Greek means wedding song—the only time the hymen is supposed to be broken is in the consummation of marriage. After the wedding night, the Jewish woman would take the sheets and bring them to her parents. If her husband ever accused her of not being a virgin when she married, they could produce the sheets as proof.

This is why during a wedding I give holy communion. That juice is a type of the blood of Christ that was shed for us, the blood of the New Covenant. We consummate marriage with the blood of Jesus.

This is why God hates divorce. Marriage is a permanent joining of a couple in a covenant. What God has joined together, He said, let no man put asunder. Now, many marriages that are not in Christ were not ordained by God. Man put it together. The justice of the peace put it together. Some hypocritical preacher put it together. God didn't. Marriage takes three—man, woman, and God.

If you are intertwined and joined for life, then you cannot break the relationship without killing somebody. God says, "I'm a covenant-keeping God. Only death can break a covenant. I cannot die because I'm God. Because I cannot die, I cannot break covenant." This is why He puts up with us, and why He put up with Israel. Israel, He said, was like an adulterous woman. He told the prophet Hosea to marry Gomer, a whore, in order to typify what Israel was and God's relationship with His people. God wouldn't divorce Israel, and didn't permit Hosea to divorce Gomer. After Gomer left, God made Hosea buy her back and stay with her. If he divorced her, she would have had to die.

This is why He won't divorce you. If He did, there would be no more hope for you. He had to give us grace. So He tells us, "If you're having trouble in your marriage, don't divorce. Reconcile. Only death can break the covenant. Men are ruining the daughters of other men, because they don't understand commitment and covenant. A man takes a woman's blood, leaves her pregnant, and goes away.

When Joseph married Mary, she was a virgin. The Holy Ghost had impregnated her. God spoke to Joseph through an angel: "This child Mary is carrying is the Savior, the deliverer." In this hour, we need some Josephs for the Marys who have been hurt through incest, rape, and molestation. Consummate that relationship. Marry her; restore her because she is a handmaiden of the Lord. Take that child and raise him. The Bible says that many saviors and deliverers will come out of Zion, but if God doesn't give us the spirit of Joseph, we will not have Marys giving birth to modern deliverers. We need Josephs to be restorers of the family and repairers of the breaches.

The only way to be a Joseph is to be connected with the Source.

Connect With the Source

When Jesus offered to share His blood in the New Covenant, many of the disciples turned away. "This is a hard saying," they said.

Jesus turned to the remaining disciples and asked, "Are you going to leave also?"

"We don't have anywhere else to go," they said. "You have the words of eternal life." They were committed to the cause. When you need a commitment, a covenant, never turn to the multitude. They will walk off and leave you. Peter and the others knew where to get the words of eternal life. They knew where the truth was. It's important to stick with the truth.

Truth is a spirit. It's not available everywhere. You need to stick to the source. David understood that Saul's kingdom did not promote truth. David remained loyal to Saul, but he got away from him. We have to be connected to something that promotes truth, honesty, and integrity.

Jesus said, "My words are spirit and truth." Stay with the truth and you won't have to worry about deceit. You won't have to worry about whether you are being manipulated. When truth is present, you shall know the truth, and the truth will make you free. Truth builds you up and frees you; it breaks shackles and loosens you.

You can see this in your own life. Since you accepted the Lord and have grown in the truth, you have been growing up, your mind has been renewed, and you've been refreshed. You see life at a different angle. The truth has freed you.

Unity in the Body

One of our basic needs is to belong, to feel loved. That's why the Body of Christ, the Church, can leave no one out. It's for everyone, and everyone has a part and a job to do. We are a body fitly joined together. I can't make it without you, and you can't make it without me. If I were to cut off my arm, my fingers would suffer. Every part in the Body of Christ is of equal importance. The same lifeblood that flows through the brain also flows to the toe.

Statement of truth. We were not born into the Body of Christ to serve a term, as in the military. We don't leave when our time is up and go do other things. Nor do we have the airport mentality, in and out. We are in the Church for the long haul.

People who have the airport mentality land and take right off again. When something is going wrong, they run to the church, get prayer, shed tears, and take right off and go back to doing the same thing. They are going to try to fly, and they are going to crash again. God is going to ground them and bring them into His hangar. He's going to over-haul them. He's not going to let them into the air until they're fixed, because He's tired of the airport mentality. It's time for men and women to have stability in their life.

Isaiah, the eagle-eyed prophet, said that wisdom and knowledge shall be the stability of our times. God is making us wise. He is giving us knowledge that is unlike the knowledge of this age. First Corinthians talks about the wisdom of this age: the rulers are ignorant, or they never would have crucified the Lord of glory. We have the wisdom that comes from God.

All of us are on the team. All of us are in the game. You might stop being a player and start being a coach. God may change your hat. He may change your anointing, your mantle, as time goes on. But you are still on the team, depending on others, and others depending on you.

Obedience to Authority

"Let every soul be subject unto the higher powers. For there is no power but of God..." (Rom. 13:1).

Jesus was subject to Pilate. Pilate said, "I find no fault in the man." To Jesus, he said, "Don't You hear me talking to You? Don't You know I have the power to take Your life?"

Jesus said, "Wait. You don't understand this. Pilate, you don't have any power or authority unless it was given you from above."

The president, the mayor, senators, governors—all are in authority because God put them there; there are certain things He needs to get done.

All power and authority come from above, so the Bible tells us to be subject to authority. This is where some churches have gone wrong—people have gotten out of order. God raises up a leader, and people will say, "I'm not going to listen to him. He's a man just like me." People think they know more than their pastors. So what if they do? I want my congregation to know more. That's why I teach them. I'm still the pastor.

I told some of them not to build a 200-seat church, because we already have a 200-seat church. They need to build a 400-seater. I'm the teacher, and they are the disciples, so they're supposed to do more than I do. This is the father mentality. They're supposed to exceed me. I am supposed to push them. I am supposed to love them. I want the church to be collecting spiritual trophies. I don't care whether I bring it home or they do.

While recognizing that no person is superior to another in God's eyes, we do need to recognize the authority God establishes. Every soul should be subject to a higher power. God is a God of order. Churches need to teach order.

David had a kingdom and everything was in order, from the top all the way down. Some of David's men could fight better than he could, but that didn't mean David had no military authority over them. His power came from God. If power is set up, it is of God. Nobody can hold a position of authority unless God has given it.

Whoever resists power resists the ordinances of God. Those who resist shall receive damnation.

Except in cases where you face a choice between obeying God or obeying man, you have no excuse for disobeying those in authority. Rulers are not here to oppose your good works. Rulers are a terror to evil works. If you don't want to fear authority, do what is good. If you do evil, you will have reason to be afraid of authority, and afraid of God who gave the authority.

In the Church, God ordained the fivefold ministry for the perfecting of the saints. Those ordained to the fivefold ministry established other positions of authority: deacons, elders, and missionaries, for example. Understand the order of leadership. The apostles chose deacons to assist them. When you see deacons choosing the pastor, run from it. That's out of divine order. God is not in it.

Leadership functions under and by authority. If you are a minister, you have to understand authority. You function under the authority delegated to you. The only way I function as a pastor is through the authority delegated to me. Jesus is the chief shepherd. I am an undershepherd. My teaching and inspiration are done under His authority.

Jesus has delegated His authority, and He's not threatened by me. He doesn't care how much my congregation loves me, or how much they build me up. When I delegate authority to the deacon, I don't care how much the people love him, or how much they love the elders. I'm not threatened. As a spiritual father, I say, "Son, go ahead," and, "God, go ahead." God will achieve what He wants to achieve, and He will get the glory.

Absalom Is a Spirit of Rebellion

Authority sharpens us. Ecclesiastes 10:10 says that if the ax is dull, you have to use more strength. You roll up your sleeves, take the ax, hit the tree, and the ax bounces off. You roll your sleeves higher and use more strength. You hit the tree and still get nowhere.

You need to sharpen the ax. Iron sharpens iron. You need me to sharpen you. I need you to sharpen me. If we don't understand authority in leadership, we will spend a lot of time hitting the tree with a dull ax and getting nowhere.

We will pass it on to the next generation, and they will do the same thing and get nowhere. If we ever get sharp through submission to God-given authority, it won't take long to cut down the tree.

In Second Samuel 18, we find David, God's beloved, the anointed king of Israel, hiding from his son Absalom, who had led a conspiracy to take away the throne of his father. The spirit of Absalom has attacked the Church continually; only a spear through the heart can defeat it. (That is how Absalom was killed.) Absalom's spirit is contrary to leadership. It doesn't understand leadership.

David had a problem with Absalom at first, because Absalom killed his own brother, then fled and stayed with somebody else. He would have killed the rest of his siblings, except that they got on their donkeys and fled. David wanted to see Absalom and restore him in the kingdom, so David called for him to come back.

Absalom wasn't interested in reconciliation. He wanted to be king, so he tried to steal his father's throne. Today, Absalom thinks he knows better than the pastor, and wants to run the church. Since he's not mature enough to run a church, he'll have to steal somebody else's.

Eventually God killed Absalom, gave the kingdom back to his father, and raised up a Solomon.

Statement of truth. God is going to bless and protect what He has anointed.

Absalom could have had the kingdom, but his heart wasn't right. God needed a Solomon.

An Absalom takes action against God's plan. It's stupid. You know he's out of God's will. You know he isn't hearing from God. He's building up his own ego. Absalom went down to the city gates. When the men of the city came by, he would butter them up. The Bible says he stole their hearts.

People who have an Absalom spirit will boast. They try to get people to follow them. If they are so great, why doesn't the Lord make them into apostles, prophets, evangelists, pastors, or teachers? The very fact that they are not called to such offices shows that they have a long way to go; God is still working on them.

But they may steal people's hearts. This is how you get church splits. Somebody doesn't agree with the pastor and steals the hearts of people. But when the dissenter finally leaves, he doesn't leave alone. He takes other people with him. That is the spirit of Absalom.

Eventually, they will get a church started. But the spirit of Absalom will turn into the spirit of Ishmael, because Ishmael is the son of the flesh. What Absalom has done, he's done through the flesh. Ishmael speaks against Isaac, the promised child, the one with the covenant promise and the anointing from God. Ishmael will speak against Isaac and soon turn into Ichabod. He is cursed.

One pastor told me that one of his preachers left the church and took 150 people with him. I was preaching at his church when the same preacher had to come back. The people who left are drifting in one by one saying, "Pastor, I'm sorry." They got confused by the spirit of Absalom. They had their hearts stolen.

The opposite of Absalom is John the Baptist. He had disciples, but when Jesus came onto the scene, John said, "I must decrease that He might increase" (see Jn. 3:30). The apostles John and Andrew were disciples of John the Baptist. When Jesus showed up, John the Baptist pointed and said,

"Behold the Lamb of God, which taketh away the sin of the world" (Jn. 1:29b). John and Andrew left to follow Jesus. John the Baptist didn't mind. He was there only to win them for Jesus.

We need to understand this in our churches. We are here to win people to the Lord. We aren't looking for people to follow us as individuals. We want them to follow Jesus.

Absalom wants people to follow him. The Absalom spirit is contrary to leadership. Absalom may perform external duty, but internally he is corrupt. He was jealous of his brother and killed him. Absalom had some Cain in him.

Absalom Is Jealous

A modern Absalom is jealous of your progress. He tries to discourage you from doing what the rest of the congregation does. If there's a midweek meeting, he'll say, "Don't you think that's a bit too much?" He'll try to turn your heart away from where God is leading you.

Absalom will try to destroy you. He doesn't want you to come into your purpose. He's afraid you might inherit the position he wants. If you are a child of God, you don't care who gets the position of leadership, as long as you are doing right. I don't care who gets the credit or who gets the glory. As long as the Kingdom is being blessed, I'm going to be blessed along with it.

Absalom incites rebellion against leadership. Absalom was the son of the king, as we are sons and daughters of the King. But Absalom was totally against what his father wanted. If the leader is going one way, then somebody with Absalom's spirit tries to influence people to go the opposite way. If the leadership is saying one thing, Absalom says the opposite. Worst of all, Absalom tries to spread that spirit throughout the congregation.

Absalom tries to magnify the leader's faults. David, like anyone else, had faults. The Absalom spirit will focus on little faults. If a leader wears red socks, or preaches too long, that's what Absaloms seize on.

Absalom will try to kill your influence among the righteous. He's always criticizing. "If I were in that position," he says, "I would do it differently." Absalom associates with people weaker than he is. He wants people who will hold onto the garbage he comes up with. He wants human garbage cans so that he can always be spreading a stink in the church. We need garbage disposals who will take all that garbage, tear it up, and send it down the drain.

Absalom and his garbage are likely to stay with you a long time. But by knowing his attributes, you can readily recognize the Absalom spirit, come against it, and destroy it. Spear it through the heart.

Leaders Need Godly Assistants

Some men of God, like Absalom, surround themselves with weak people, people they can run. Jethro told Moses, "Choose some men who fear God—able men, men of truth who hate covetousness. Put these men in authority." These men would keep Moses straight. "Moses," Jethro said, "if you mess up, these men will get you back in order."

However, Moses still needed to teach them. He had to show these men what to do, and he had to be doing it himself.

David also had men to keep him in order. When David said, "We are going to number Israel," Joab said, "I don't want to. I'll do it. But you are wrong, David. God said not to do it. Can't He raise up thousands to fight for Israel?"

David went ahead and conducted the census. God killed 70,000 men.

"I told you you were wrong," Joab said.

On another occasion, after Absalom was killed, David was weeping and weeping. Joab said, "David, listen. Absalom was going to kill us. If you don't get up from there and stop crying, then all of us are going to leave you."

David got up, pulled himself together, went back to Jerusalem, and started reigning again.

Leaders need men and women like Joab around them—people of truth, who fear God, who hate covetousness, and who will keep their leader in line.

If a leader surrounds himself with deacons and assistant pastors who are whoremongers and who steal, then he will be shaky, too. If they are doing it, the pastor will say, "I can do it." But if he has honest people, people of truth, surrounding him, it will be hard for him to fall.

A leader needs people to whom he can delegate responsibility, who can act with his authority. Some ministers in my church come on Sunday only. They are solid men. They are living holy. But they kill their influence with the people by coming to only some of the services. Then, when I go out of town, the people don't have as much confidence in them as they have in me. But I try to build them up.

It is important to be faithful, and I will build them up, because I'm not threatened. God has established this work, and I will build up the elders, the ministers, and the deacons. I will pat them on the back and teach the congregation to respect and honor them.

When I was under another pastor, I was careful to be there to support him. When the pastor went out of town, I was able to step in and have as much influence as the pastor. But I knew where to channel the influence. I knew that God could not unlock my dreams unless I unlocked the dreams of my pastor. Although I had influence in the congregation, I built up the man of God who was over me.

A Leadership Test

Every leader will face seasons of flourishing and seasons of dryness. By the way he dealt with the crisis concerning Korah, Moses showed that he had what it took to be the leader of Israel. He illustrated characteristics that a godly leader needs to have.

Are you willing to stand with God's man when the whole congregation is against you, as Aaron did with Moses?

Are you willing to be falsely accused? The people blamed Moses for the death of Korah and the other rebels. Are you willing to be lied about, even when you know you are full of truth and a person of integrity?

Are you willing to pray, intercede, and supplicate for the very ones who lie about you, misunderstand you, and falsely accuse you?

Are you willing to be misunderstood even when you know you're right?

Are you willing to be identified with Jesus not only in flourishing times, but when He is being nailed to the cross?

Are you willing to stand before God on behalf of the very people who are attacking you? You offer the incense of prayer that smells sweet in God's nostrils. How far are you willing to go?

David too exemplified the leadership traits exhibited by Moses. When he was right, he stood his ground, yet he was always willing to sacrifice himself for the good of the people he served.

To be a man or woman of God, it's not enough to oppose Absalom. You have to be willing to follow God's calling no matter where it takes you. You have to be a David.

Chapter 6

In the Hope of His Calling

*C*ease not to give thanks...The eyes of your under-standing being enlightened; that ye may know what is the hope of His calling, and what the riches of the glory are of His inheritance in the saints* (Ephesians 1:16-18).

The Williams' translation says, "...by having the eyes of your heart enlightened so that you may know what the hope is to which He calls you. How gloriously rich God's portion in His people is."

You are not only called, but chosen; not only chosen, but elected.

Nobody and nothing can damage, hurt, or kill you until God is finished with you. Let them lie about you, talk about you, criticize you, delay you. It doesn't matter. God takes what was meant for our harm and uses it for our good.

Keep your eyes, mind, heart, and will focused on the reason you are on earth, in the Kingdom of God, and connected with the Body of Christ at this time. You are here on purpose. God placed you in this generation for a reason. He hand-picked you for this time. No matter what you are going through, no matter what is on your mind, what trouble you have, how many valleys you've been in, no matter what valley you're in right now, you were selected by God for this time.

You have not begun to see the best of you. You have not yet prayed your greatest prayer, not yet worked your greatest miracle. You have not yet sung your greatest song, nor tapped into the greatest portion of your anointing. But it is coming.

Coming Prosperity for the Church

Having set us here with a purpose, God would not leave us ignorant of that purpose. His people are a knowing people. Those who know their God shall be strong and do exploits.

Knowledge is like light in the darkness. Jesus called us the light of the world. Light chases away the darkness. The only way the world is going to see in this hour is through us. Our knowledge of God—our intimate relationship with Him—will give light for the world to see.

So far, the world has seen the Church as a poverty-stricken, religious, cold, dry people. The world is going to see more in this hour because God has taught us principles. He is going to sow us like seed, to transfer our knowledge of Him to the world. Therefore, we must be careful not to fall back into the system of this world. The world says, "Get all you can and hold onto it." It tempts us to hold onto money tighter than we hold onto God.

But God is sowing saints who are going to blossom and become illuminators. When the world sees us, it is going to see a glorious Church. We are going to shine with the glory of riches. Under the system of God, the Church is going to be like the kingdom of David.

David and his men took cities. David was able to give a huge amount of money to the house of God. That was out of his own wealth, and that wasn't all of it. He gave out of his abundance. When the world looked at David's kingdom, they saw something glorious, something magnificent, something splendid. They knew that God was with David; David had the evidence to prove it.

When people look at the Kingdom of God in the year 2000, the saints of God are going to be as prosperous materially as they are spiritually. John's saying will come to pass: "Beloved I wish above all things that thou mayest prosper and be in health, even as thy soul prospereth" (3 Jn. 2). The world is going to be afflicted with AIDS and other diseases. But God is going to keep His Word: "...I will put none of these diseases upon thee..." (Ex. 15:26). We will walk around healthy, prosperous, and spiritual. When the world sees us, they are going to see the splendor and glory of God. "Out of Zion, the perfection of beauty, God hath shined" (Ps. 50:2). Zion is the Church. This is going to happen. If I am a man of God, if I am a prophet, it is going to happen. I sense it in my spirit.

As this thing comes upon the Church, don't draw back into the system of the world. We need to hate the system of this world. We should hate the things God hates. "Do not I hate them, O Lord, that hate Thee?" (Ps. 139:21a). Jesus told us to be in the world but not of it. We don't belong to the system. If Jesus had belonged to the system, He could have called 12 legions of angels to rescue Him. His Kingdom is not of this world, but it is going to take over this world. "The kingdoms of this world are become the kingdoms of our Lord, and of His Christ..." (Rev. 11:15b).

This is why finances are being taught so heavily in the Church right now. There is a harvest God wants to bring forth in every believer's life. A transference is going to take place. People on the cutting edge are going to see it sooner.

Some Christians haven't even heard of this. We are sent to inform them, to instruct them, to let them know what God is getting ready to do. They don't know what God wants them to do, and they are just sitting there waiting.

I recently preached at a church where they were having a pastor's anniversary. I didn't intend to talk about tithing; it just came out. "How many in here tithe?" I asked.

The preacher sitting behind me said, "I don't tithe. That's Old Testament."

So I took him through the Old Testament, into the New Testament, and had his head spinning. I think he was ready to tithe when I finished. I had planned to cancel that preaching engagement, but the Holy Spirit had impressed upon me to go. I didn't know I was going to face a pulpit full of preachers with a poverty mentality.

They took up an offering, and collected one thousand $1 bills. I took the dollars and held them up. "See these things?" I asked. "They are spirits." I didn't want them. I took up another offering and gave it all to the pastor. I didn't have a mind to do that when I first went there, but sometimes God changes your plans.

Pastors all over this land need to learn about the way Christians are supposed to handle money, because the Church is going to take over this nation. "Righteousness exalteth a nation..." (Prov. 14:34).

God Reveals His Intentions

Sometimes circumstances blur our vision and make us lose our sense of direction. God has caused our hearts to see, so that we might know why we are here. He will not leave us punching the air or going in circles. The world might not understand what God is doing, but we understand. God enlightens us that we might know. He will always inform us of what He is about to do before He does it. "Surely the Lord God will do nothing, but He revealeth His secret unto His servants the prophets" (Amos 3:7). The Church is going to know ahead of time before God does anything.

Throughout history, this has been the pattern of God. Before God sent a famine on the land of Egypt, He informed Joseph. Before God brought Israel out of Egypt, He told Moses. God is going to inform His servants, who will tell the people of God, so that nothing will come as a surprise. We will never be caught off guard.

This is why the Spirit of God said, "He that has ears, let him hear what the Spirit is saying to the Church." God's messages to seven churches are recorded in the Book of Revelation. He commended them and warned them. In certain areas, they had to tighten up their lives. People will mess up, then repent, and then feel that same tendency to mess up again. God will warn them: "You messed up. I forgave you. Go back and do that no more."

God will always give a warning before sending judgment. This is the way God operates. We know the truth, and the truth shall make us free. Before the Lord Jesus Christ comes back, we will have knowledge. He will come as a thief in the night, but there will first be a great falling away and a great coming together all at the same time. We're not going to know the exact date, but we will know the season. In the air we can sense a happening.

Right now we sense a need to evangelize. It's time to really reach out. Many of us sense that, but sometimes we disregard it. Down in our spirit we know. Every now and then,

God sets off an alarm in us and tells us it's time to do something. When He does, we need to go full force into doing it; it is going to work because it is in the timing and season of God.

Things We Know

"For I know that my redeemer liveth, and that He shall stand at the latter day upon the earth" (Job 19:25).

"When I cry unto Thee, then shall mine enemies turn back: this I know; for God is for me" (Ps. 56:9).

"For I know that the Lord is great, and that our Lord is above all gods" (Ps. 135:5).

"I know that the Lord will maintain the cause of the afflicted, and the right of the poor" (Ps. 140:12).

"I know that, whatsoever God doeth, it shall be for ever..." (Eccles. 3:14).

"The people that do know their God shall be strong, and do exploits" (Dan. 11:32b).

"Then shall we know, if we follow on to know the Lord..." (Hos. 6:3).

"We know that all things work together for good to them that love God, to them who are the called according to His purpose" (Rom. 8:28).

"Know ye not that ye are the temple of God...?" (1 Cor. 3:16).

"Know that your labour is not in vain in the Lord" (1 Cor. 15:58b).

"We know that if our earthly house of this tabernacle were dissolved, we have a building of God, an house not made with hands, eternal in the heavens" (2 Cor. 5:1).

"I know whom I have believed, and am persuaded that He is able to keep that which I have committed unto Him against that day" (2 Tim. 1:12b).

"We know that we have passed from death unto life, because we love the brethren…" (1 Jn. 3:14).

"We know that the Son of God is come, and hath given us an understanding, that we may know Him that is true…" (1 Jn. 5:20).

A Message for Today

God wants us to warn people that it is time to be a doer and not just a hearer of the Word. It's time to do something with God. It's time to do the impossible. Let's do something the world says we can't do. Let's touch something the world says is untouchable. Let's reach something the world says is unreachable.

They see us, but they don't see the invisible force with us, which is God Almighty. If God is for us, who can be against us? Greater is He who is in us than he that is in the world.

That's why Paul said, "I can do all things." There is nothing you can't do, nothing you can't conquer with Christ. "I can do all things through Christ which strengtheneth me" (Phil. 4:13). You would be surprised how powerful that Scripture is if we believe it. If we have that belief down in our soul, down in our spirit, we can do anything.

Statement of truth. Every calling is important. Don't minimize your calling; maximize your potential.

Not everybody can be David. But all the tribes joined with David (see 2 Sam. 5:1). We can all be a part of what God is doing with and for His anointed. I can't be David, but I sure can be a part of what God is doing. I can't be Paul, Peter, Bartholomew, or Matthew, but I can be Jeff. In being Jeff, I can be a part of what God is doing in the earth at this moment, and I'm going to be all that I can be. Every day I'm striving to tap into that potential in me that has yet to surface.

Myles Munroe has said that with all we have accomplished and all we have done, God is looking down on us and saying, "I have more than that planned for you."

Knowledge Through Old Testament Types

God gave us examples in Scripture to let us know how He works and what He is going to do today.

God gave us Melchizedek, Abel, Enoch, and Noah's ark.

Enoch passed from earthly life into eternal life without going through death, to typify the resurrection.

Noah's ark was a type of Jesus Christ. There was only one way in. There was only one window, which faced upward. God shut the door, which was a type of salvation, because it was what brought Noah, his family, and all the animals through the flood. It took them beyond the judgment of God into the Promised Land. Jesus does the same thing for us.

Abel was a type of the Lord Jesus Christ, who gave God an acceptable sacrifice.

Melchizedek was a type of the Lord Jesus Christ, who had no beginning and no ending. Melchizedek just came on the scene. The Bible doesn't describe his lineage. He was the king of Salem, the king of peace.

Joseph was a type of Christ. He went down to Egypt and saved Egypt from the famine that would come.

Moses was a type of Christ. He said, "God shall raise up a prophet like unto me" (see Deut. 18:15).

When God gave Moses the design of the tabernacle, He told him, "Be sure you do it according to the pattern." Jesus was the heavenly pattern, the heavenly tabernacle. There was only one way into the tabernacle. Even the white fence around the tabernacle was a type of Jesus. It was plain on the outside; there was nothing to attract you to the inside. But the inside was decorated with gold and silver. Jesus had "no form nor comeliness...no beauty that we should desire Him" (Is. 53:2b). People can't understand how wonderful Jesus is from the outside; you have to get to know Him.

The gold inside the tabernacle speaks of the deity of God. The silver speaks of redemption. The brass speaks of His judgment. The altar on which they sacrificed animals typified Jesus our sacrifice.

The brazen laver was where the priests washed themselves before going into the holy of holies. That typified Jesus as the water that washes away our sins.

The candlestick typified Jesus, the light of the world.

The bread typified Jesus, the bread of life.

The altar of incense typified Jesus our high priest offered up for us.

The veil itself was the Lord Jesus Christ. When Jesus died on the cross, the veil was torn from top to bottom, signifying that salvation came from above. The angels tore the veil while the body of Jesus was being torn for the sins of the world, giving us access from the holy place to the holy of holies. Once the veil was taken away, not only could the high priest go into the holy of holies—everybody could.

Inside the holy of holies was the ark of the covenant.

The mercy seat signified the mercy of God. On the mercy seat the priest sprinkled blood, which typified Jesus' blood sacrificed for our sins.

Under the mercy seat was the law. The blood had to be sprinkled on the mercy seat so that God wouldn't see the broken law. If He saw the blood first, He couldn't see the broken law, signifying that Jesus covers and forgives our sins. The mercy seat was the place of atonement. *Atone* means "cover." God not only covers our sin, He removes it as far as east is from west.

Also under the mercy seat was the golden pot of manna, and the rod of Aaron that budded. God had taken a dead, dry stick and made flowers grow on it; it typified the resurrection of Jesus Christ. The manna in the wilderness turned rotten after one day, except on the Sabbath. How did the manna in the golden pot last for years? Because it was in the presence of the Lord.

Everything about the tabernacle spoke about Jesus Christ.

For the Kingdom of God to really work, everybody has to function together according to their individual callings. *Togetherness* is the key word in the Kingdom of God. It hurts the Church when everybody is in their own little corner, doing their own thing, and hollering, "I have the truth!" Nobody has the whole truth. It takes all of us together to get the job done.

Jesus taught us something about that with the disciples. Several times He told them how to catch more fish. When that happened, the disciples had to call for help, because there were too many fish for them to handle. No one man can do it. It takes others helping. It takes the fivefold ministry and everybody working together.

Learn From David's Mighty Men

David's kingdom was a type of the Kingdom of God. The men who came to him strengthened themselves. If you are strong, and you stand with somebody who is strong, it makes you stronger. In establishing David's call, they established their own.

If you turn to God, you will be strengthened. Those who sit in David's cave at Adullam come out mighty men and women. We need to catch the spirit of David's mighty men (see 1 Chron. 11:10). They were champions. They excelled. They were powerful and victorious. They had a warrior spirit. They were men of renown.

But the most impressive thing about them is that they acted according to the Word of the Lord concerning Israel. It doesn't matter how great a man or woman seems—people who can't act according to the Word of the Lord are not great in the sight of God.

The Gadites were another class of people who joined David. Imitating them will help you function in the hope of your calling.

The Gadites "separated themselves unto David into the hold to the wilderness men of might, and men of war fit for the battle, that could handle shield and buckler, whose faces were like the faces of lions, and were as swift as the roes upon the mountains" (1 Chron. 12:8). Gad was the son of Jacob who, in the long run, could overcome a troop (see Gen. 49:19).

The Gadites were an overcoming people, a people who knew victory. A people who knew only to overcome. We are overcomers, too. We have overcome the world by our faith.

Revelation 2 and 3 encourage us to be overcomers, offering promises to those who overcome.

Learn From the Gadites

They separated themselves unto David. This represents leaving the works of the flesh. You can't function properly in the Kingdom of God if you dabble in the works of the flesh. You cannot be an effective Kingdom builder if you succumb to the lusts of the flesh. Separate yourself unto Jesus, the seed of David. Leave the works of the flesh alone. You can't mix spirit and flesh. You mustn't be lukewarm. We have many Kingdom people trying to be lukewarm. Be hot or cold.

They were men of might. They were able to raise the productive power of the nation. Whatever David was doing, these men were able to take it to a higher level. Can you take the productive power of your church to another level? God will show you things to do, people you can reach out to.

They were fit for the battle. They weren't trying to get ready; they were already skillful and prepared for physical and spiritual warfare. Your times in Adullam and in the wilderness will leave you prepared for the battle ahead.

They could handle shield and buckler. They were versatile. They could attack as well as defend. The shield speaks to us of faith. Versatile people can usher or greet or clean the bathroom or cut the grass or visit the hospital. We can say, "God, use me any way You want to." My high school didn't have many football players; a lot of us had to learn both defensive plays and offensive plays, and be in the game for the whole sixty minutes. It made us versatile.

They had faces of lions. This speaks to us of praise and worship. You can be as powerful and confident as a lion when you pray.

They were as swift as roes. We need to be quick to answer God's call. Don't hold back waiting to see if someone else will answer. Run to the battle.

We can learn from all these traits of the Gadites. David had many types of men and women joining him, all for the furtherance of the kingdom. He needed all kinds. And whatever your gift, it has a place in the Kingdom of God. Function in the hope of your calling, whether you are called to help a David establish a kingdom, help a Solomon build a temple, help a Deborah lead God's people into warfare, or help a Nehemiah build a city.

Be active and dynamic. Be energetic and diligent. Be reliable and wide awake. Be alive and industrious. Be vigorous and alert. Function in the hope of your calling, and no matter whom you're helping, function in the hope of their calling.

Unlocking Your Dreams

The only way to unlock your own dreams and visions is to unlock somebody else's.

Joseph dreamed that the sun, moon, and stars bowed down before him. He dreamed that he was in the field with his brothers, and that their sheaves bowed down before his. Joseph's brethren called him a dreamer.

In Potiphar's house, Joseph began to unlock Potiphar's dreams. Once Joseph arrived, Potiphar became successful. But Joseph's dreams were still not unlocked. In fact, he ended up in prison. There he unlocked the butler's dream and the baker's dream. Soon Joseph was unlocking Pharaoh's dream.

You may be only one relationship away from the palace. Keep unlocking people's dreams; the day is coming, and it is not very far off, when God is going to unlock yours. When you unlock someone's dream, that person will often turn around and unlock yours.

Statement of truth. The person whose dream you unlock will turn right around and unlock yours. God has a way.

Jacob unlocked Laban's dream, and Laban said, "What can I give you?" It's a principle. Unlock other people's dreams, and they will unlock yours.

I Am Me

In all the world there is no one else exactly like me. Everything that comes out of me is solely mine, because I alone chose it.

I own everything about me—my body, my feelings, my mouth, my voice, all my actions, whether they be to others or to myself.

I own my visions, my dreams, my hopes, my fears.

I own all my triumphs and successes, all my failures and mistakes, because I own all of me.

I can become intimately acquainted with me. By so doing, I can love me and be friendly with me.

I know there are aspects I do not know, but as long as I am friendly and loving to myself, I can courageously and hopefully look for solutions to the puzzles and for ways to find out more about me.

However I look and sound, whatever I say and do, and whatever I think and feel at a given moment in time is authentically me.

If later some parts of how I looked, sounded, and felt turned out to be unfitting, I can discard that which is unfitting, keep the rest and invent something new for that which I discarded.

I can see, hear, feel, think, say, and do.

I have the tools to survive, to be close to others, to be productive, and to make sense and order out of the world, of people, and of things outside of me.

I own me.

And, therefore, I can engineer me.

I am me, and I am OK.

Get that down in your spirit, and you will know that God has placed things in you to help the Kingdom of God.

Chapter 7

The Importance of People

You are important to the purpose and the will of God. You fit into His plan. You are one of the living stones who are joined together as a habitation for the Spirit of God. You would not be here if God did not have a plan for you.

Part of His plan is to restore you. "I will restore to you the years that the locust hath eaten..." (Joel 2:25). "There shall be showers of blessing" (Ezek. 34:26b). This is the day and the hour for restoration. God's going to rain blessings on us in some tremendous ways.

Some time ago, I was in Charleston, West Virginia, preaching about restoration. As I read from the Scripture about God raining blessings on us, the people went wild. I didn't know why. After the service, Bishop Jakes said that a visiting preacher had spoken on the same passage of Scripture the previous night. That preacher was from Cortland, Ohio, and we had never spoken to each other. But God had us preaching the same message, and the people knew something was going on. It was a sign from God that He is going to rain blessings on us.

God Exalts His People

God will confirm His anointing on us.

Now Hiram king of Tyre sent messengers to David, and timber of cedars, with masons and carpenters, to build him an house. And David perceived that the Lord had confirmed him king over Israel, for his kingdom was lifted up on high, because of his people Israel (1 Chronicles 14:1-2).

God exalts a leader because of his people. In restoring His people, God has a place He wants to take them. So He exalts a man of God to get them there. The leader and the people work hand in hand. They reflect glory on each other.

The more people in the kingdom, the more honor the king has; the king will be destroyed if he lacks people (see Prov. 14:28). So God will always raise up a man of integrity to lead His people. They need a man of honesty and dignity—a man with a clean heart.

David was that man, and he had great honor because of his people. He wanted them—as a group and as individuals— to be exalted. This is what happened in David's kingdom. David had men there who were mightier than he was, who could use the sword better, but when David was exalted, every man under him gained prestige and glory, too.

There is something in God's people that He wants to spread around the world. The people determine how great their king will become, and how far their kingdom will reach. At our church, we had a brothers' meeting every night for a while, and the faith of those men reached around the nation. People who visited the church went out and told others about the men's meeting. When I went to Grand Rapids, all I heard about was the men's meeting in my own church and the strength of that ministry. People came in, saw the core of the ministry, and duplicated it in other places. Often, they did a better job than our own church. That's proper: the disciples should always do a better job than the master. Those people caught the vision of the men's group at our church; they caught the vision and ran with it.

"Where there is no vision, the people perish..." (Prov. 29:18). It's also true that where there are no people, the vision perishes. Not only should the pastor be a visionary, but the people need to catch the vision, too. Every vision needs legs in order to go anywhere. The legs are the people who will carry out the vision.

Our Choices in God's Plan

Our choices govern our destiny. It is vitally important that we choose rightly. Our will is governed by the higher law of God. All our choices must first be consistent with His Word.

You may exercise your will by jumping off a building, but you will still be governed by a higher law, the law of gravity. You can jump off, but you will get hurt. You have to submit to the higher law. This is why Jesus said, "Not My will, but Your will be done."

You can speed down the highway and get someplace faster, but you will probably get a ticket or get hurt or hurt somebody else. There is a higher law that governs. God has given us choices, but He's given us a higher law within which to make our choices. We make our choices while submitting to the laws of God and the laws of the land. If we break the higher laws, we need to get back under submission to them.

The thief on the cross had broken the higher laws. He knew he was in trouble and had just about run out of time. "Lord," he said, "remember me when You come into Your kingdom." He didn't just want Jesus to think about him. He realized that he had been in God's plan from the foundation of the world. God had chosen him for a purpose, and he needed to get back to that purpose. "I got off track," he was saying. "When You come into Your kingdom, bring me back up to what I should have been, to what You had planned for me in the beginning."

Sinners need to realize that they were chosen by God before the foundation of the world. They don't know what was in store from the beginning, and don't know how to be restored to God. God has to rain on them. He will restore them to what they used to be.

We didn't always know that we were a part of Jesus in the beginning. We didn't know that we were chosen. When we got saved, God remembered us. He reconnected us, and put us back where we used to be. Now we are here to fulfill His purpose.

The thief on the cross teaches us what we need to do: We need to ask of God. God is ready to answer and act. God is concerned about people. He cares about us. He loves us. People prompt God to do the amazing and the miraculous. He will do something amazing and miraculous for you, because He loves you and is concerned about you. God is involved with your welfare.

God's Heartbeat

That is God's heartbeat: people. God is love. But in the beginning, when there was nobody but God, there were no people toward whom He could show His love. God created us in His image so that He could express His love. Love isn't love until you give it away.

God so loved the world that He gave His only begotten Son. Christ loved the Church and gave His life for it. We need an object toward which we can express our love. Love is no good if it's kept inside. You can be walking around smiling, but if you don't express your love, nobody will know that you are a creature of love. You have to demonstrate it.

Statement of truth. Because God is involved with people, He invests special abilities and skills in the lives of a particular people. Because you are a member of His Church, His people, He has invested abilities and skills in you. You are chosen by God, to be exalted individually and as one of His people.

God said, "I didn't choose you because you were many; I chose you because you were few, and I set you above all the people of the earth." This is why He told Israel, "When you get into this land and dwell in goodly houses and eat of vineyards you didn't plant, and drink from wells you didn't dig, don't say that the power of your own hand has obtained this. Say it is the Lord who gives you the power to get wealth, because He loves you."

God is saying the same thing to us, and the people in David's kingdom are an indication of who we are supposed to be. First Chronicles 12 lists the people who joined David, and who were exalted with him. The children of Ephraim were men and women of great reputation, and held in high esteem. A Christian held in high esteem can walk into the midst of a conversation of sinners, and they will stop cussing because they hold him in high esteem. When you walk in,

God walks in, and when God steps in, it shuts the mouths of fools.

Learn From the Children of Issachar

The children of Issachar "had understanding of the times." If you have understanding of the times, you know what you are supposed to be doing in this hour. In our church, we have morning worship at 11 o'clock; people who have understanding of the times are going to be there at 11 o'clock. Some people don't understand the times. You'll see the door swing open at 11:30 because some people don't understand what time it is. They don't understand that they have missed 30 minutes of worship and praise in the presence of the Lord. You'll see people walk in at 12 o'clock because they don't understand what time it is.

People who want something from God and want to render praise to God get up early on Sunday morning, because they understand what time it is. They don't want to miss the move of God and the anointing of God. People who don't understand what time it is won't even show up at church.

If you know what time it is, you will be seeking knowledge of God. Knowledge of God renews us into the image of Jesus Christ. The more you learn about the Word, the more you learn about God, and the more you look like Him. When you know that the sons and daughters of God are having a meeting, you will want to be there. You see the day of the Lord at hand, so you want to be where God is. How foolish it is to miss a gathering when He is in the midst of it. But we will let some simple thing stop us.

Whether it is Bible study, church, or a special meeting, the devil plants excuses in our minds. If we hear that there's going to be a revival for five days, right off the bat our minds say, "I'll make three of them. That's better than making two." We start from a position of compromise, instead of devotion. We start out lukewarm, instead of hot.

The sons and daughters of the King will be there to hear what He is saying. They will walk out transformed.

In God's presence we will acquire wisdom. People cannot believe I am 32 years old. They look at me and shake their heads. "Never in my life have I seen such wisdom," they will say. "How old did you say you are?" The key to my life is that I go to every gathering I can. I know that the Son of God is there.

A while ago I was invited to a banquet in New Orleans. I didn't feel like going. But I went, and God told me some things I never would have gotten unless I had been in that banquet. At any gathering of the church, you are in the right place at the right time with the right people. When the King is in the gathering, He will speak to you.

If you are like Issachar, you will pay attention to the Spirit telling you what time it is. "Stand still." "Know that I am God." "Worship Me." "Dance." "Shout." "Run." The children of Issachar are people who know what the Church ought to do right now. People who don't know need to get with somebody who does know. Issachar is going to get the job done.

They are a working people who can bear burdens in the heat of the day. At night no man can work, because he would stumble. When Issachar sees the sun rise, he knows it's time to get up and get to work.

Other people lose track of time. They think they have all the time in the world to do what God wants them to do, so they miss out on what God is doing. Issachar knows that every time the clock ticks, we're closer to leaving this place. Issachar knows that God has given us a certain amount of time to do what we need to do. Soon I'm going to stand before Him. If I haven't done what He wants me to do during this time, I'm not going to hear "well done."

Issachar will hear "well done." Their knowledge of God caused Issachar to do great exploits. What exploits are you doing? Knowledge is power. People who know their God are strong. How are you using that power? So many weak saints walk around saying, "I can't make it. I can't do it. I can't hang in there." The Bible says, "Be strong, and whatever your hands find to do, do it with all your might" (see Eccles. 9:10). Be a doer of the Word.

Learn From the Children of Zebulun

They went forth to battle. This signifies that they were not a fearful people. We're in a war, and God needs people like the children of Zebulun. You have to enlist the right people.

Gideon had the wrong people at first. God said, "You have to get rid of them. People drinking water like a dog—they're going to get somebody killed. Send them home. People who are scared—send them home. They'll get somebody killed. As a matter of fact, they'll start killing each other." Out of thirty thousand people, Gideon wound up with three hundred, and they destroyed a nation.

If the children of Zebulun had been fighting with Gideon, they would have been in the three hundred. They would have made the final cut. They were expert in war. They were specialists. When you are a specialist, it means that whatever you do, you do it with excellence. If you are a prayer warrior, you do it with excellence. People will say, "If

I can just make it there and they lay their hands on me, I'm going to be all right."

This is what the woman said who lost her son (see 2 Kings 4:8-37). She told her servant, "Go to the man of God and say, 'The son you have given me is dead.'"

The man of God sent his servant. "I don't want the servant," she said. "I don't know whether he is an expert. I want the man of God himself." The man of God went there, lay upon the son, breathed on him, and life came back into him.

We not only need to be experts, we need to be versatile. The children of Zebulun were versatile. Whatever it took to win, they used it. Our instruments of war include prayer, fasting, praise, worship, and money. Sometimes what we have to do will require money. Sometimes it's going to take prayer. God might say, "I want you to pray all night," or, "I want you to fast for three days." We have to be versatile.

"God," we must say, "whatever You want, I'll give it to You. I'm Yours. Use me until You use me up. Set me on fire. Burn me up." The children of Zebulun could keep rank. They knew how to submit. It brought glory to God and to the team as a whole.

The children of Zebulun were not of a double heart. They were not flaky. We don't need flaky people in the Kingdom of God. We need people who are single-minded and stable. The children of Zebulun were not double-tongued, double-faced, hypocritical, or tricky. They were steadfast, immovable, sincere, straight up. They were solid men and women who could be trusted. Trust is something people don't just give you. You have to earn it.

Learn From the Children of Dan

They, too, were "expert in war"; they didn't act like amateurs. They were professionals; they had finesse. We need to be formed into mature warriors. God doesn't want amateur Christians. We need full-time professionals in the house of God. I'm not talking about people getting a salary. I'm talking about people who are committed to God's work 24 hours a day, seven days a week.

Professionals can handle responsibility. They can take the hassle. An amateur can't. The first time the devil says, "Boo," they fall to pieces, and we have to patch them up. An amateur gets into spiritual warfare and can't take it, and quits.

The professionals, the experts in spiritual warfare, will see the victory.

Getting and Using the Overflow

"A faithful man shall abound with blessings" (Prov. 28:20a). How do you get that abundance of blessings? The first thing is to recognize where it comes from.

Wherefore David blessed the Lord before all the congregation: and David said, Blessed be Thou, Lord God of Israel our father, for ever and ever. Thine, O Lord, is the greatness, and the power, and the glory, and the victory, and the majesty: for all that is in the heaven and in the earth is Thine; Thine is the kingdom, O Lord, and Thou art exalted as head above all. Both riches and honour come of Thee, and Thou reignest over all; and in Thine hand is power and might; and in Thine hand it is to make great, and to give strength unto all (1 Chronicles 29:10-12).

Having recognized the source of abundance, the next step is to seek God and His will. Don't seek to be rich (see 1 Tim. 6). If you are going to be rich, let it come on you. Don't run after it; let it run after you. "Be rich in good works" and trust "in the living God." Keep in stride, and help those around you to keep in stride also, not to miss His will. Wives and husbands need to support each other, and encourage each other. In times of temptation, especially when doing the right thing will have negative consequences from other people, a husband and wife need to help each other to do what is right.

If you are rich in good works, that is more valuable than any wealth you could amass on earth. If you are rich in good works, and trust in the living God, then when you need help you will have it.

David blessed the Lord in front of the congregation; he acknowledged that all good things come from God. But he didn't try to grab them. God made him king in His good time, and David didn't try to circumvent that. As a result of his faithfulness, chasing God instead of chasing riches, David had God at his side. "I was in the midst of my enemies," he said, "and I cried unto the Lord. The Lord heard my cry and He thundered from heaven as a mighty man. Smoke came out of His nostrils. He caught the cherubim and rode on the wings of the clouds. And He stepped on the earth and He crushed His enemies" (see 2 Sam. 22:7-18; Ps. 18:6-17).

Fire came out of His mouth because He heard David's cry. What's He going to do when He hears your cry? I dare you to cry to Him and find out. Call Him. He will thunder like a mighty man. Smoke will come out of His nostrils. He won't take the next flight; He doesn't have to sit in the airport waiting for the next plane. He has cherubim ready. He'll jump on them and say, "Come on, let's go! I heard My son cry. I heard My daughter cry."

As David said, everything in heaven and earth is His. What do you have to worry about? Sometimes we need divine assistance, and it will come. But often, we don't realize that we have what we need right next to us.

When Samuel was alive, a lot of times Saul wouldn't listen to him. But once he was gone, Saul went looking for him. He went to the witch of Endor and said, "Could you bring back my Samuel?" When God allowed Samuel to come back, Samuel said, "God still rejects you."

God had given a commandment: Let every witch be killed. Saul didn't listen to the prophet when he could have, and ended up going to somebody he should have killed. The next day, Saul went into battle and was killed himself.

Everything good will come from God's hand. If we don't have the things we want, then maybe we don't appreciate what we have. Saul didn't appreciate Samuel while he had him. If we try to get the things we want from any place except God's hand, we will end up outside God's will. People turn to the occult, as Saul did, or to stealing or cheating to get what they want. They go against God's higher laws. When you do that, just as when you try to break His law of gravity, you're going to fall.

If you want an abundance of blessings, it has to come from His hand. If you're in relationship with God, you're already in His hand, and nobody can pluck you out of it. If you're in the hand that will make you great, you'd be foolish to walk out of it. You're already in the hand that gives strength unto all.

Faithfulness is the key to receiving His abundant blessings. Those who are faithful to Him will receive more. He'll give it to you when you are ready. You will have to start small, be faithful with what you've been given, and then you will receive more.

First You Have to Die

Every tree started from a seed, and for the tree to grow, somehow, some way, that seed had to get into the earth. We start as seeds. To grow and become great we must submit ourselves to the earth. If you don't die to self, you are not going to grow, because God will not command the earth to release you until you die.

When a seed submits itself to the earth, it doesn't just grow up. It grows down first. You die and then you begin to grow down. When you are dead to yourself, that's when people begin to say you're a religious fanatic. "You go to church all the time. You need to slow down some." Those words don't affect dead men. You give ten percent of your wages and an offering on top of that to the church. "You're giving all your money to the church," they say. If you are dead, those words don't mean anything. Since you are dead, they don't see that you are growing down. You must grow down first in order to grab hold of the earth.

Then God will tell the earth to release you and let you grow up. After that you will break forth out of the earth. You stayed faithful while everyone kept talking about you and saying you were nuts. Now they will see you spring up out of the earth. They will see truth stand up now. No matter what they say, they won't be able to shake you, because you grew down first before you grew up. Now you have roots. The wind can blow, rock you back and forth, but you're not going anywhere because you have grown down first. It can rain on you now, but all that rain is going to do is make you grow up.

You can't stop a tree once it has some roots and is growing up. I've stepped on little trees in the woods and have seen them spring right back. They had roots.

Maturity

When you are mature, the wind might shake your fruit off, but you will just produce more. Let the wind blow all it wants. If some fruit get knocked off, it's going to feed somebody. Next year, you're going to produce more fruit, and the following year you'll produce even more. As long as God lets you stay on the earth, you'll go on producing fruit.

God has an overflow for us, and He's going to give it to us. The main requirement is faithfulness. A faithful man shall abound with blessings.

You turned to God when you were in distress, in debt, and discontented. In the cave of Adullam, He taught you, trained you, and gave you rest. He turned you into a mature Christian who is ready to do His will. You have the understanding of the times, and are expert in warfare. He has turned you into somebody who can do something for Him, and who can build up those around you. Now you just need to stick right beside Him and live in the abundance of His grace. Fulfill the purpose He has for you, and grow rich in good works until you hear Him say, "Well done."

Advertisements

Other
Destiny Image titles
you will enjoy reading

BENT NAILS AND CHIPPED BRICKS

by Jeffrey Reed.

Have you ever felt ignored or stepped on by life? This book will encourage you whether you're a "bent nail" or a "chipped brick." Everyone has a place in the Kingdom that God is building! Discover how you can turn your setback into a comeback—and reach out for God's blessings!

Paperback Book, 128p. ISBN 1-56043-265-9 Retail $6.99

WOMAN, THOU ART LOOSED!

by T.D. Jakes.

This book offers healing to hurting single mothers, insecure women, and battered wives; and hope to abused girls and women in crisis! Hurting women around the nation—and those who minister to them—are devouring the compassionate truths in Bishop T.D. Jakes' *Woman, Thou Art Loosed!*

Paperback Book, 210p. ISBN 1-56043-100-8 Retail $9.99

NAKED AND NOT ASHAMED

by T.D. Jakes.

With a powerful anointing, Bishop T.D. Jakes challenges us to go below the surface and become completely and honestly vulnerable before God and man. In relationships, in prayer, in ministry—we need to be willing to be open and transparent. Why do we fear? God already knows us, but He cannot heal our hidden hurts unless we expose them to Him. Only then can we be *Naked and Not Ashamed*!

Paperback Book, 156p. ISBN 1-56043-835-5 (6" X 9") Retail $11.99

CAN YOU STAND TO BE BLESSED?

by T.D. Jakes.

You ask God to bless you and difficulties arise. Why? This book will release the hidden strength within you to go on in God, fulfilling the destiny He has for you. The way to this success is full of twists and turns, yet you can make it through to incredible blessing in your life. The only question left will be, *Can You Stand to Be Blessed?*

Paperback Book, 196p. ISBN 1-56043-801-0 Retail $9.99

Available at your local Christian bookstore.

Internet: http://www.reapernet.com

Prices subject to change without notice.

Exciting titles
by Myles Munroe

UNDERSTANDING YOUR POTENTIAL

This is a motivating, provocative look at the awesome potential trapped within you, waiting to be realized. This book will cause you to be uncomfortable with your present state of accomplishment and dissatisfied with resting on your past success.

Paperback Book, 168p. ISBN 1-56043-046-X Retail $8.99

RELEASING YOUR POTENTIAL

Here is a complete, integrated, principles-centered approach to releasing the awesome potential trapped within you. If you are frustrated by your dreams, ideas, and visions, this book will show you a step-by-step pathway to releasing your potential and igniting the wheels of purpose and productivity.

Paperback Book, 182p. ISBN 1-56043-072-9 Retail $8.99

MAXIMIZING YOUR POTENTIAL

Are you bored with your latest success? Maybe you're frustrated at the prospect of retirement. This book will refire your passion for living! Learn to maximize the God-given potential lying dormant inside you through the practical, integrated, and penetrating concepts shared in this book. Go for the max—die empty!

Paperback Book, 196p. ISBN 1-56043-105-9 Retail $8.99

IN PURSUIT OF PURPOSE

Best-selling author Myles Munroe reveals here the key to personal fulfillment: purpose. We must pursue purpose because our fulfillment in life depends upon our becoming what we were born to be and do. *In Pursuit of Purpose* will guide you on that path to finding purpose.

Paperback Book, 168p. ISBN 1-56043-103-2 Retail $8.99

POTENT QUOTES

Dr. Myles Munroe believes that every day is a classroom, every experience a lesson, and everyone we meet a teacher. In this collection he has taken the life-changing potent sayings and lessons he has learned and powerfully encapsulated them in quote form. Here you'll learn about leadership, ability, potential, and purpose—all in *Potent Quotes*.

Paperback Book, 80p. ISBN 1-56043-161-X (6" X 4") Retail $4.99

Available at your local Christian bookstore.

Internet: http://www.reapernet.com

Prices subject to change without notice.